understanding jewish prayer

understanding jewish prayer

BY
JAKOB J. PETUCHOWSKI

ktav publishing house, inc.
new york
1972

לאלישבע

Table of Contents

INTRODUCTION

The subject of Jewish prayer may be approached from a number of different angles, all of which contribute to a better understanding of this important element of Jewish life. There is, for example, the *aesthetic* approach, which addresses itself to the *structure* of the Jewish worship service. There is the *historical* approach, which endeavors to trace the *development* of the Jewish liturgy from its rather simple beginnings to the elaborate devotional literature available to the modern Jew. There is the *exegetical* approach, which seeks to fathom the different levels of *meaning* of the prayers which have gone into the making of the Jewish worship service.

Yet, underlying the materials thus studied, there is the phenomenon of *prayer* itself, the act of man's addressing himself to God. This is both a datum of religious experience and a task for theological understanding. Moreover, since man, outside of philosophical constructs and oversimplifying ideologies, is never man in the abstract, but a concrete, specific individual, who stands within a concrete, specific religious tradition, there is room for an investigation of how the *Jew* is experiencing *Jewish* prayer, and of what the *Jewish* theological tradition has to say on the subject.

That investigation is the task we have set ourselves in the following pages. The six chapters of Part One deal with various concepts, of both a theological and a halakhic (legal) nature, which Tradition has bequeathed to the modern Jew, and with the modern Jew's problems and possibilities of making those concepts his own—in theory as well as in practice. Here we discuss the dialectics of spontaneous devotion and fixed liturgical forms, the concept of prayer as an "obligation," the theological problem involved in addressing specific and detailed requests to an all-knowing God, and, not least, the even more fundamental problem of modern man's ability to pray in the first place. Here, too, we try to come to terms with some of the "practical" problems which have been widely discussed in connection with modern Jewish worship. There is, for example, the role of the Hebrew language in Jewish prayer, and there is the question about the degree of hospitality which the synagogue service can offer to the kind of innovation which is designed to make the worship experience more "interesting" and "entertaining" —without ceasing to be what it was meant to be: *Jewish* worship.

Those first six chapters will, we trust, reflect a consistent outlook on, and understanding of Jewish prayer. They are one man's view, based, we hope, on an adequate knowledge of the main thrust of the classical sources, and informed by an awareness of today's Jewish reality. No uniformity of outlook, however, is intended in Part Two, which is designed as a kind of symposium, and brought together in the nature of an anthology. In that part of the book, the reader is meant to be introduced to a *variety* of reactions to the Jewish worship experience, and to *differences* in theological approach. A certain amount of repetition is inevitable here; but the reader will note—with interest, we hope—how some of the same classical sources are dealt with in different ways by different authors.

The seven chapters of Part Two, therefore, do not necessarily reflect, in each and every comment and interpretation, my own views; nor, for that matter, would the seven authors included in Part Two necessarily agree with everything said by the author of Part One—or, again, with one another. Obviously, no attempt has been made to "censor" or otherwise change the seven chapters of Part Two to make their contents conform more to the outlook of the author of Part One.

Still, such differences in religious (and, sometimes, even political) outlook as are reflected in these pages must not be exaggerated. All the authors represented in this volume share a positive commitment to Judaism, all of them believe in the value of prayer, and all of them move within the same theological universe of discourse. And I am happy and fortunate to be able to number all seven authors of Part Two among my friends. In an age of increasing polarization, that is something for which I am profoundly grateful.

An outstanding Israeli scholar is reported to have made the following comment: "With the people, with whom I can talk, I cannot pray together; and with the people, with whom I can pray together, I cannot talk." That, happily, is *not* true of the eight authors brought together within this volume. They do, as it happens, represent different interpretations of Judaism. Some of them may be more eager than others to be identified by such different labels as "Orthodox," "Conservative," and "Reform." But they *do* talk together; and they *can* pray together. Most of them have, in fact, already done so on occasion.

Indeed, it may be regarded as the chief criterion of selecting the material presented here that it was all written by men who can understand one another—in spite of differences in theological emphasis, and who can pray together—notwithstanding differences in liturgical predilections.

Another criterion was the inevitable limitation of space. A number of essays, which—both in terms of the first criterion and in terms of the contribution which they make to the understanding of Jewish prayer—would have merited inclusion, had to be left out in order to keep this book within manageable proportions. In this connection, we would like to draw the reader's attention to two monographs which he may want to take up after completing the reading of this volume: Eliezer Berkovits, "Prayer," in Leon D. Stitskin, ed., *Studies in Torah Judaism*. New York, Yeshiva University Press and Ktav Publishing House, 1969, pp. 81–189; and Louis Jacobs, *Jewish Prayer*. London, Jewish Chronicle Publications, 1955.

A word has to be said about the transliteration of Hebrew terms. There are about as many systems of transliteration as there are people transliterating Hebrew words into English. Every system has its advantages and its disadvantages; and every author has his good reasons for adopting his particular system. It stands to reason that it would have been an impossible task to harmonize the transliterations of eight different authors—particularly since, in part, we are dealing with material which had been previously published. The reader, therefore, should not look for a uniform system of transliteration in this volume; and we apologize for any possible inconvenience. An attempt has, however, been made to bring some kind of consistency into the transliteration of Hebrew words in the Notes. This, we trust, will facilitate the scholar's consulting of the sources quoted.

"May the graciousness of the Lord our God be upon us;
Establish Thou also upon us the work of our hands;
Yea, the work of our hands, establish Thou it."

(Psalms 90: 17.)

Jakob J. Petuchowski

Cincinnati, Ohio,
Tu Bishevat, 5732 / January 31, 1972.

ACKNOWLEDGMENTS

We are grateful to the following authors, editors, publishers and holders of copyright for granting us permission to reproduce previously published materials:

The Association of Reform Rabbis of New York City and Vicinity, before whom the main part of Chapter Three, "Cult, Entertainment and Worship," in a somewhat different form, was delivered as The 1970 Benjamin A. Tintner Memorial Lecture, and who published the original lecture in pamphlet form.

The Central Conference of American Rabbis, from whose *C.C.A.R. Yearbook*, Volume LXXVII (1967), the major part of our Chapter Six, "Can Modern Man Pray?," is here reprinted.

Professor Abraham Joshua Heschel and the Rabbinical Assembly of America for permission to use as Chapter Seven, "On Prayer," an article by Professor Heschel which appeared in *Conservative Judaism*, Vol. XXV, No. 1, Fall 1970.

Professor Steven S. Schwarzschild for contributing a newly revised version of "Speech and Silence before God," as Chapter Eight, and to the Editor of *Judaism*, in which an earlier version of this essay appeared in the Summer 1961 issue.

Professor Ernst Simon and the B'nai B'rith Hillel Foundations for permission to reprint Chapter Nine, "On the Meaning of Prayer," which originally appeared in Alfred Jospe, ed., *Tradition and Contemporary Experience*. New York, Schocken, 1970.

Professor Gerald J. Blidstein and the Editor of *Judaism* for permission to reprint Chapter Ten, "The Limits of Prayer," which originally appeared in the Spring 1966 issue of *Judaism*.

Rabbi Dudley Weinberg for contributing Chapter Eleven, "The Efficacy of Prayer," and to the Jewish Chautauqua Society for permission to reprint it from their Pamphlet No. 2.

Professor Eliezer Berkovits and the Editor of *Judaism* for permission to reprint Chapter Twelve, "From Temple to Synagogue and Back," which originally appeared in the Fall 1959 issue of *Judaism*.

Mr. Milton Himmelfarb and the Editors of *Commentary* for permission to reprint Chapter Thirteen, "Going to Shul," which originally appeared in the April 1966 issue of *Commentary*.

J. J. P.

A BIBLIOGRAPHICAL NOTE

While this book is not intended either as a history of Jewish liturgy or as a guide to the structure of the Jewish worship service, there are two rubrics of the liturgy to which constant reference is made throughout these pages. One of them is "The *Shema* and its Blessings (or Benedictions)." The other is the prayer variously referred to as "The Eighteen (or Seven) Benedictions," "The Eighteen-Prayer," "The *Amidah* (= the prayer recited in a standing posture)," or, particularly in the Rabbinic sources, quite simply as "The Prayer." The Jew who is in the habit of praying regularly knows those rubrics well. But for the benefit of the student, who may lack such a personal acquaintance with the Jewish prayerbook, we offer here the page references in four widely used editions of the Jewish prayerbook, in the hope that he will familiarize himself with those rubrics to gain a better understanding of what is being said about them in this volume. Page references are given to the following:—

Daily Prayer Book, ed. Philip Birnbaum. New York, Hebrew Publishing Co., 1949. Orthodox. Referred to as *Birnbaum*.

Sabbath and Festival Prayer Book. The Rabbinical Assembly of America and The United Synagogue of America, 1946. Conservative. Referred to as *RA*.

Union Prayer Book. Newly Revised. Volume I. Cincinnati, The Central Conference of American Rabbis, 1940. Reform. Referred to as *UPB*.

Service of the Heart. London, Union of Liberal and Progressive Synagogues, 1967. British Liberal. Referred to as *SoH*.

(1)   "The *Shema* and its Blessings"
      (a) Evening Service
      Birnbaum, pp. 191–197.
      RA,   pp. 15–19.
      UPB,   pp. 13–17.
      SoH,   pp. 29–35.

      (b) Morning Service
      Birnbaum, pp. 71–81.
      RA,   pp. 87–95.
      UPB,   pp. 125–141.
      SoH,   pp. 39–43.

(2)   "The Prayer of the Eighteen (or Seven) Benedictions"
      (a) Weekday
      Birnbaum, pp. 81–97.
      RA,   pp. 230–237.
      UPB,   pp. 320–326.
      SoH,   pp. 44–56.

      (b) Sabbath
      Birnbaum, pp. 265–273, 349–359,
                   391–405, 449–459.
      RA,   pp. 21–15, 96–101,
                   137–145, 169–176.
      UPB,   pp. 19–25, 125–141.
      SoH,   pp. 68–73, 129–134.

      (c) Festival
      Birnbaum, pp. 585–597, 609–625.
      RA,   pp. 29–33, 146–156.
      UPB,   pp. 193–201, 225–243.
      SoH,   pp. 312–321.

Part One
DYNAMICS AND DOCTRINE

JAKOB J. PETUCHOWSKI

1

Chapter One

SPONTANEITY AND TRADITION

Kavvanah is one of those Hebrew words which elude a simple one-word translation. It means "direction," "attention," "concentration," "devotion," and "inwardness."[1] It means the free outpouring of man's heart before his Father who is in Heaven. It means the spontaneous expression of our deepest concerns and our highest aspirations. For the Rabbis, *kavvanah* was the absolute prerequisite of true prayer. "Prayer without *kavvanah* is like a body without a soul."[2] The nature of such a prayer of *kavvanah* cannot be predetermined. Both the occasion which calls it forth and the state of mind of the person who utters it are decisive here. Moses, on one occasion, prayed for forty days and forty nights, interceding on behalf of his people; and his prayer was answered.[3] Yet, on another occasion, Moses' prayer on behalf of his sister consisted in all of five Hebrew words; and that prayer was answered, too.[4] On neither occasion was Moses likely to have used a prayer which someone else had written for him. His prayers were prayers of pure *kavvanah*; and so were the prayers of all the other biblical figures who are portrayed as having prayed. There was no prayer book in the biblical period. There was no actual *book* of prayers in the Rabbinic period. In fact, the Rabbis were opposed to the writing down of prayers, considering those who did write down prayers to be as reprehensible as those who would burn the Torah.[5] Not until the ninth century C.E. do we get a written Order of Service for Jewish worship.[6]

But the prayer of *kavvanah* is not only something we read about in the Bible. It is something which practically all of us engage in at one time or another. Something good happens to us, or something we had dreaded does not happen; and, quite spontaneously, we burst out saying, "Thank God!"—perhaps without even realizing that the two words we have uttered

3

constitute a prayer. Sometimes, indeed, such a prayer of
kavvanah may have no actual words at all. It may just take
the form of an anguished "Oh!" or an exhilarated "Ah!"—as a
kind of shorthand in which we express ourselves in the
continuous presence of the "Hearing Ear."[7]

None of the appurtenances, the paraphernalia and the
machinery of organized religion are necessary to facilitate the
uttering of such prayers of *kavvanah*. There is no *a priori*
reason to doubt the word of the man who excuses his absence
from synagogue services by saying: "I do not need the
synagogue to pray; I can commune with God in nature." He
may well be right—even though there are many who are
probably somewhat less than honest in claiming that ability.
Surely, the great psalmists, who saw "the mountains skipping
like rams, and the hills like lambs" (Psalms 114:4), who
heard "the sea roar and the floods clap their hands" (Psalms
98:7f.), who discovered that "the heavens declare the glory of
God, and the firmament showeth His handiwork" (Psalms
19:1), and who then proceeded to bequeath unto us the world's
greatest religious poetry—surely, *they* managed to commune
with God in nature. We can hardly imagine them getting
their inspiration in the pews of a house of worship, or behind
the typewriter of some liturgy committee, trying to meet a
deadline for a new edition of the prayer book.

Whoever, therefore, knows the Bible, whoever is acquaint-
ed with some of the private prayers which the great virtuosi
of prayer have contributed to our heritage, from the scholars
of Talmudic days through the charismatic leaders of
Hasidism, whoever, in fact, has ever expressed his own
gratitude or concern with or without words—he will have to
admit the truth of the claim that the institutions of organized
religion are not an absolute prerequisite of prayer. But it is
equally true that the possibilities of prayer are not exhausted
by the intermittent occasions which prompt us to utter
private prayers of *kavvanah*. The latter represent but *one*
dimension of prayer. There is also another.

Prayer, if we think about it carefully, is actually a supreme
manifestation of impertinence, of *chutzpah*. But such is the

unique Jewish stance towards God that, according to one view
in the Talmud, "*Chutzpah,* even against God, is of avail."[8]
The underlying impertinence of prayer is the tacit assumption that man has but to open his mouth, and God will hear
his prayer. Man does not deal in this fashion with his own
human authorities. The ordinary citizen has little hope of
ever communicating directly with the head of his government. At best, he will be heard by a subordinate official on
some lower echelon of the administration. Yet man takes it
for granted that he may have an audience with the Sovereign
of the whole Universe, the Holy One, praised by He, at any
time he chooses. That is the great daring, the *chutzpah*
underlying the act of prayer.

What we have just expressed in a style imitating that of the
ancient Rabbis could also be formulated in a somewhat
different manner. Prayer, we might say, presupposes that
finite, mortal, limited man can address himself to eternal and
infinite God, that human heart and divine mind can be attuned
to each other. Such a thought does not come easily to all men.
Indeed, the constantly reiterated pleas in the liturgy that God
hear our prayers, and that He answer our petitions, would
seem to indicate that even the experienced virtuosi of prayer
in our millennial tradition have not been unaware of the
theological as well as the psychological difficulties in making
one's own the psalmist's simple affirmation that "the Lord is
nigh unto all that call upon Him,/To all that call upon Him in
truth./He will fulfil the desire of them that fear Him;/
He also will hear their cry, and will save them." (Psalms
145: 18-19.)

The theological problem involved in opening up a conversation with God would be all the greater for us today if we were
the first human beings in history to make an attempt at
prayer, if that conversation had not been initiated long before
we came upon the scene. But that is precisely the advantage
enjoyed by members of the historic faith-communities that
they are merely *continuing* a conversation with God which
had been begun by their ancestors centuries and millennia
ago. And that is particularly true of the faith community of

Israel, the Jewish people. When a Jew prays, it is not as
though a finite human being suddenly took it into his head
that he may attune his mind to the infinite mind of God.
Rather can he build, as it were, upon the contact which had
been established long, long ago. The faith community of
Israel today stands in prayer before the God of Israel even as
it has stood before Him ever since Sinai, and even as its
Patriarchs, Abraham, Isaac and Jacob, had already turned to
Him when our people was as yet but a single tribal family.
The prayer I address to "our God and God of our fathers, God
of Abraham, God of Isaac, and God of Jacob," is indeed the
prayer which *I* offer; but it is also a strand within that
tapestry of prayer woven by generations upon generations of
my ancestors, and joined to those many other strands which
my fellow Jews in all parts of the world are contributing at
this very moment. In other words, standing before God in
prayer, I do not stand alone. I stand in the company of my
people, a company both visible and invisible, spanning space
as well as time.

Community prayer, then, adds another dimension to
prayer, a dimension which is not accessible to him who would
go off alone into the woods to commune with God in nature. It
certainly does not invalidate such individual prayer. It
supplements it. And for many, although perhaps not for all, it
makes prayer itself easier. It helps to make manifest the
presence of the Holy One, whom the psalmist describes as
"enthroned upon the praises of Israel." (Psalms 22: 4.)

Yet for community prayer to be *community* prayer, there
will have to be certain features which represent a recognizable constant, linking one worship experience to another. A
community is not a haphazard crowd made up of stray
individuals. It is a group of people with something in common.
That is why Jewish community prayer would cease to be
Jewish community prayer if today's worship service were to
be something totally and entirely different from yesterday's
worship service, or last week's, or last year's, or that of a
hundred years or two thousand years ago. Similarly, the Jew
who travels from Bombay to Chicago must find some

elements, known to him from Bombay, in the Chicago service, just as the Jew who moves from New York to Tel Aviv must find familiar elements in the Tel Aviv service. Otherwise it would make no sense to speak of a Jewish community prayer at all, and the advantages of community prayer, which distinguish it from individual prayer, would be lost.

This need for a recognizable constant leads to the gradual crystallization of fixed parts of the worship service which remain, with very minor local modifications, always and everywhere the same. Thus a prayer *tradition* comes into existence, a routine element which gives community worship its "fixed" aspect. It is what the ancient Rabbis called *keva*, the fixed, the routine, the traditional.

But affirming the necessity of the *keva* aspect of Jewish community worship, simple as it may sound, and obvious as it may seem to be, really leads to a very serious dilemma. If the highest form of prayer is spontaneous prayer, the prayer of *kavvanah*, how can *keva*, a fixed prayer routine, be countenanced? This dilemma was already faced by the early Rabbis, and can, perhaps, best be illustrated by a statement of one of them.

Rabbi Simeon said: "Be careful in the recitation of the *Shema* and in the Prayer; and, when you pray, do not make your Prayer a matter of fixed routine *(keva)*, but an entreaty for mercy and grace before the Omnipresent One, praised be He."[9]

The dilemma underlying this statement will be more clearly seen when it is realized that, when Rabbi Simeon speaks about "the Prayer," it is not prayer in general to which he is referring, but a very specific prayer, the Prayer of the Eighteen Benedictions. This Prayer of the Eighteen Benedictions (or "of the Seven Benedictions" on the Sabbath and festivals) was, by its very nature, a *fixed* prayer which the Rabbis felt *obligated* to recite at least twice every day—while, in the course of time, it became the virtually universal practice to recite it *three* times a day. If ever, therefore, there was cause to call a prayer "fixed routine" *(keva)*, the Prayer of the Eighteen Benedictions must have automatically qualified

for that description. Yet it is precisely in connection with that
prayer that Rabbi Simeon utters his warning not to make it a
matter of fixed routine!

Similarly, Rabbi Eliezer said: "If one makes his Prayer a
matter of fixed routine (keva), his Prayer is not an entreaty
for grace."[10] But, given the obligation to recite the fixed
Prayer daily, what alternatives were there? Apparently, some
of the later Rabbis thought it possible to invest the prayer of
keva with kavvanah. Discussing what Rabbi Eliezer could
have meant by speaking about keva, some Rabbis thought
that keva is the prayer of anyone who feels that the prayer
rests like a heavy burden upon him, while others thought that
keva was any prayer not uttered "in the language of entreaty."[11] Obviously, therefore, in the view of those Rabbis, it
must have been possible to recite the fixed prayer without
feeling weighed down by the obligation of having to do so, and
to recite it with that feeling of urgency and devotion which is
characteristic of the "language of entreaty."

In our own days, Professor Abraham Joshua Heschel has
attempted to show that a fixed prayer can be recited with
kavvanah. If we use words in our prayer, says Heschel, we
must realize that words, even our own words, are really
external to us—only slightly less external than the words
which others have written for us. But, to the extent to which
man may derive inspiration from the use of words in the first
place, to that extent man may, on occasion, feel that the words
which the great men of prayer have composed for him may
even be more adequate to his needs than the words for which
man may have to grope himself.[12]

According to Heschel, therefore, and he has the weight of
Tradition behind him, it is not at all impossible to use the
traditional and fixed words without feeling that a heavy
burden is thereby imposed upon us, and to use those words
with all the inwardness and all the urgency of the "language
of entreaty." Jews have done it for millennia; and it can still
be done. Indeed, if we take into consideration the experience
of those religious denominations which have substituted the
minister's extempore prayer for a printed prayer book, or if

we are familiar with the so-called "creative services" of non-Orthodox Jewish youth groups in America today, we may well conclude that the weekly extempore prayer becomes so stylized and so repetitive that it tends to grow stale long before the same fate overtakes the polished and expressive phrases of a classical liturgy.

That, however, is only one part of the story. We must also consider the historical setting in which Rabbis Simeon and Eliezer uttered their warning against making the Prayer a matter of "fixed routine." The talmudic discussion of Rabbi Eliezer's statement, from which we have already quoted, continues by giving us the definition of "fixed routine" (keva), suggested by both Rabbah and Rav Joseph. Those Rabbis define keva as the prayer "of anyone who is unable to say something new in it."[13] That is to say, in the days of Rabbah and Rav Joseph, and all the more so in the days of Rabbi Eliezer and Rabbi Simeon, even the "fixed" Prayer of the Eighteen Benedictions was not nearly as "fixed" as it was to become with the much later invention of printing.

As late as the fourteenth century, David Abudraham, a Spanish-Jewish liturgist, was able to say that "you will not find a single place in the world where the Eighteen Benedictions are word for word identical with the way in which the Eighteen Benedictions are recited anywhere else. Rather are there those who add words, and those who omit words."[14]

What was "fixed" in the early Rabbinic period was the number of the benedictions to be recited, and, somewhat later, the overall topic of each benediction and, in general outlines, its concluding eulogy (chatimah). But about the fixed nature of the sequence in which those benedictions were to be recited there was as yet no unanimity in the talmudic period.[15] Certainly, the actual wording of the benedictions was not "fixed" by the early Rabbis. Hence the worshipper was afforded an opportunity of "saying something new" each time he prayed. To this day, the practice in Orthodox and Conservative synagogues of reciting the Eighteen Benedictions silently before they are repeated aloud by the prayer

leader harks back, in part, to the procedure of synagogues in
the talmudic period, where, in the absence of written and
printed prayer manuals, the prayer leader was given time to
arrange his thoughts and to choose his words before leading
the congregation in the Eighteen Benedictions.

Moreover, even when a "traditional" wording of the
Eighteen Benedictions later crystallized, it did so, to begin
with, in two different versions—one in Palestine, and one in
Babylonia. And, while the invention of printing and the
subsequent availability of printed prayer books have somewhat toned down the discrepancies noted by Abudraham in
the fourteenth century, they have by no means made for a
uniform liturgical rite even among those Jews who consider
themselves to be adherents of Orthodoxy. The wording of the
Eighteen Benedictions is still not identical in the various
"Orthodox" rites. Variations in wording still distinguish the
Eighteen Benedictions of the Spanish and Portuguese Jews
from the Eighteen Benedictions of the German and Polish
Jews, even as the Hasidic Jews use a third version, and the
Yemenites a fourth. The number of benedictions is the same,
the ideas expressed are the same, even the sequence of the
benedictions is now the same; but variety still obtains when it
comes to the actual wording!

This being the case, we can understand how a Rabbi Simeon
and a Rabbi Eliezer could, at one and the same time, take for
granted the obligatory and fixed character of the Eighteen
Benedictions, and yet insist that the worshipper inject his
own feelings and expressions into it, treating that prayer as
anything but *keva*. Such was the balance struck between
kavvanah and *keva* in the early Rabbinic period. Yet the very
fact that, for more than a thousand years now, we have had
books of prayer points up something else as well. It underlines
the importance of realizing that the balance struck by the
early Rabbis between *kavvanah* and *keva*, between the
respective claims of spontaneity and tradition, was a balance
which met the needs of their own times, and of their own
times only. That balance had to be struck anew time and
again in the history of Jewish prayer; for, in that history, we

can discern the operation of a basic law of liturgical
development: "One generation's *kavvanah* becomes another
generation's *keva*." An illustration will help to make this
clear.

Already within the talmudic period itself, the Prayer of the
Eighteen Benedictions had become somewhat crystallized in
structure and in content, and had become the *congregational*
prayer *par excellence*. It was felt, therefore, that there was a
need for the individual to be allowed some time, within the
framework of the public worship service, to express his own
thoughts and feelings in his own words. Thus, after the
recitation of the Eighteen Benedictions, the Order of Service
called for a period of private prayer, variously called "words,"
"entreaties," or "the falling with the face to the ground"
—which latter was originally the worshipper's posture for his
private prayer after the Eighteen Benedictions had been
recited in a standing position.

Now, nothing is easier than to affirm the *principle* of
private prayer, and the superiority of spontaneity over
tradition. Nothing, however, is harder than finding the
appropriate words for actual communion with God. It is not
surprising, therefore, that the disciples of the great Rabbis
should have made a point of finding out what kind of prayers
their masters were uttering during that period of the worship
service which was devoted to private prayer. A number of
those private prayers of the Rabbis are recorded in the
Talmud, each one introduced by the formula, "Rabbi X, after
his Prayer (of the Eighteen Benedictions), said the following."

Thus, Rabbi Eleazar would pray: "May it by Thy will, O
Lord our God, to make to dwell in our lot love and brotherhood
and peace and friendship. Mayest Thou make our borders rich
in disciples. . . ."[16]

Rabbi Chiyya would pray: "May it be Thy will, O Lord our
God, that our Torah be our occupation, and that our heart
may not be sick nor our eyes darkened."[17]

Rav would pray: "May it be Thy will, O Lord our God, to
grant us long life, a life of peace, a life of goodness, a life of
blessing, a life of sustenance, a life of bodily strength, a life in

which there is fear of sin, a life free from shame and
confusion. . . ."[18]

About a dozen such prayers are brought together by the
Talmud in this passage. Among them is the prayer of Mar, the
son of Ravina: "My God, keep my tongue from evil and my lips
from speaking guile. May my soul be silent to them that curse
me, and may my soul be as dust to everyone. Open my heart in
Thy Torah. . . ."[19]

Several of those private prayers were ultimately utilized in
various rubrics of public worship. For example, Rav's private
prayer, with some minor verbal changes, became a part of the
liturgy used in connection with the announcement of the New
Moon in Ashkenazi congregations; and that only less than two
centuries ago.[20] But by far the most popular prayer was the
private prayer of Mar, the son of Ravina, "My God, keep my
tongue from evil. . . ." Since the ninth-century prayer book
of Rav Amram Gaon, this originally private prayer of Mar
has been a part of every Jewish worship service. It is recited
immediately after the Eighteen Benedictions—in that part of
the service which was originally reserved for the prayer of the
individual. In other words, the *kavvanah* of Mar, the son of
Ravina, has become the *keva* of later generations.

What, then, happened to the free prayer of the individual
which was to follow the Eighteen Benedictions? That rubric of
"entreaties" was, at first, merely postponed until after the
prayer of Mar. But, in the course of time, that "free period,"
too, was invaded by words fixed by tradition, words which, no
doubt, were, at one time, the free outpouring of the hearts of
individuals. Fixed words for the "entreaties" are a relatively
late phenomenon in the history of Jewish liturgy and, in this
rubric, there are the greatest variations among the different
traditional rites. Yet the extent of this invasion of *kavvanah*
by *keva* is dramatized by the two printed pages of "entreaties"
in Philip Birnbaum's edition of the *Daily Prayer Book* for the
daily service, and the six pages of "entreaties" for the service
on Monday and Thursday![21] Free prayer still has its place in
the traditional Jewish worship service. But it is more or less
restricted to the time before the beginning, and the time after

the end of public worship. There are also some optional elaborations of some of the Eighteen Benedictions—as when the worshipper wants to mention the sickness of a specific person in the benediction dealing with God's healing powers.[22]

It would seem to follow from this illustration that not only did one generation's *kavvanah* become another generation's *keva*, but also that the dialectic between spontaneity and tradition has, in the course of the centuries, invariably led to the ultimate supremacy of the latter. That is true, but only to a certain extent. It is true, for example, that—at any rate, until the invention of printing and the availability of printed prayer books—the Jewish prayer book has undergone a constant process of additions, and that, with very minor exceptions, there has never been any omission. Whatever was admitted into the liturgy, remained there to stay—even if the very purpose of introducing the prayer in the first place had long since become devoid of meaning. Thus, the Orthodox Jew to this day prays for the welfare of the heads of the Babylonian academies,[23] even though those academies closed their doors a thousand years ago. Yet, at one time, that prayer certainly met an existential need. Every period of Jewish history left its imprint upon the prayer book. Biblical psalmists, Pharisaic interpreters, Rabbinic sages, medieval bards, commentators and philosophers, the mystics of ancient and of more recent times—they all had their share in the formation and growth of the Jewish liturgy. And so did the history of local communities, perpetuated in a host of liturgical *minhagim* (local customs). Indeed, so rich in historical reminiscences is the Jewish prayerbook that it is an invaluable aid in the study of Jewish history, even as it has kept alive the historical consciousness of countless Jews who did not make Jewish history a subject of specific study.

The invention of printing, as was noted, inhibited the further growth of the liturgy, although, here and there, some relative latecomers still managed to gain entrance. For example, the service of "Welcoming the Sabbath"[24] was contributed by the mystics of sixteenth-century Safed, in the

Land of Israel; and the memorial prayer, *El malé racha-mim*,[25] entered the liturgy as a result of the Chmielnicki massacres in seventeenth-century Poland.[26] But, even without the interruption of the process of growth brought about by the invention of printing and subsequent liturgical standardization, it is difficult to conceive of an uninhibited continuation of that process. The sheer amount of material accumulated over the millennia had already resulted in worship services of a duration which made the sustained attentiveness and devotion of the worshipper difficult, if not altogether impossible. It was left to nascent Reform Judaism in the nineteenth century (followed, to a certain extent, by Conservative Judaism) to bring the dialectics of *kavvanah* and *keva* into flux again. This was accomplished not only by introducing new *kavvanah* elements, but also by venturing to jettison some of the old *keva*. Of course, by doing so, Reform Judaism departed from a very old tradition, and had to bear the brunt of being considered innovative.

Yet—and such is the irony inherent in the dialectics of *kavvanah* and *keva*—not only the nineteenth-century Reformers had to bear that brunt. Whoever, in the course of the millennia, had contributed his own prayers of *kavvanah*—even without touching the inherited *keva*—also had to bear the brunt of being a "reformer." So much of what had become *keva* was, at one time, *kavvanah* and, as such, had to fight for its right of existence by the side of such *keva* as was already extant.

For, when all is said and done, *adding* to the inherited liturgy is as much a "reform" as *omitting* from it. Both the adding and the omitting are ways of indicating that the inherited tradition, in its crystallized form, no longer meets the religious needs of a new generation. The true religious conservative takes the attitude of "What was good enough for my grandfather is good enough for me!" It is the religious liberal who, on occasion, feels impelled to "sing unto the Lord a *new* song." Judaism has always been blessed with both its religious conservatives and its religious liberals, and that is why new additions to the Jewish liturgy have always been marked by fierce religious struggles—some of them quite as fierce as were the struggles in the nineteenth century when, for a change, the struggle was about omissions as much as it was about additions.

It is, moreover, another irony that some of the nineteenth-century battles were fought about the omission of some of the very elements the original introduction of which was so fiercely resisted by the religious conservatives of an earlier age. In this connection, we are thinking primarily of the liturgical poetry of the Middle Ages. Some of the greatest legal authorities of Judaism had either objected to certain types of synagogal poetry or to the introduction of poetry as such, since it represented an "interruption" in the hallowed sequence of the classical prayers.[27]

As it turned out, the people's *kavvanah* was allowed to overrule the legal objections of the conservatives, and synagogal poetry became an integral part of medieval Jewish worship. The people were also allowed to have the *Kol Nidre* formula at the beginning of the Atonement Eve service, even though some of the heads of the Babylonian academies in the ninth and tenth centuries were violently opposed to this practice, describing it as a "foolish custom" (*minhag shetut*).[28] And the people's *kavvanah* was able to set aside many a rabbinic caution in connection with the popular observance of the feast of *Simchat Torah*.[29]

The long history of *keva* is, therefore, itself an eloquent testimony to the power of *kavvanah* in the evolution of Jewish liturgy. This, too, has to be borne in mind when one concludes that, in the dialectics of *kavvanah* and *keva*, the latter has, in the long run, usually gained supremacy. After all, the law of Jewish liturgical development, "one generation's *kavvanah* becomes another generation's *keva*," is reversible, too. It would be just as true to say that much of what is one generation's *keva* had been the *kavvanah* of earlier generations!

Withal, the worship experience is not, in and of itself, identical with an appreciation of Jewish history and of the workings of a law of liturgical development. The claims of

Tradition may be felt by some of our more unbound spirits to be an undue restriction; and the attempt to be in line with the familiar Jewish liturgical landmarks in space and in time may, on occasion, put a damper on attempts to emulate the latest fashions and fads in the entertainment world. One does have to pay a price for remaining within the system of checks and balances represented by *kavvanah* and *keva*.

What, then, does one get in return for paying that price? Quite simply, the ability to pray as a Jew, the opportunity of experiencing a dimension of prayer which is accessible only to the faith community of Israel standing together before the God of Israel, and the proud awareness that one is personally involved in the task of weaving the millennial tapestry of Jewish prayer out of the strands of spontaneity and tradition.

Chapter Two
OFFERING AND OBLIGATION

In common parlance, when "prayer" is mentioned, the reference more often than not is to something a man *feels* like doing, to something man is *moved* to do. The sight of a breathtaking landscape may move us to exclaim: "How great are Thy works, O Lord!" A situation of distress and suffering may move us to cry out: "Save us, O Lord!" A personal or a national deliverance may make us feel like thanking God, and that feeling is then translated into such words as "Thank God!" Technically, we may call the three types of prayer just mentioned: Adoration, Petition, and Thanksgiving; and they are indeed the basic ingredients of Jewish prayer. Of course, in the illustrations given, we have reduced those elements to their most simple components. In actual practice, particularly within a synagogal setting, the wording is liable to be much more elaborate, the sentiments more fully developed. In the previous chapter we have already indicated the value of that added dimension to prayer which comes from knowing ourselves to be at one with the faith community of Israel, and which, therefore, imposes on us the need to temper our own *kavvanah* with a certain amount of communal *keva.*

Yet such is the nature of Jewish prayer that, in addition to the limitless times a man may pray when he feels so moved *(tephillat reshut),* Tradition also knows of *obligatory* prayer *(tephillat chovah).* By uttering the prayer of that latter category, the Jew is not only giving vent to his own feelings and emotions. He is, in fact, fulfilling a *mitzvah,* a divine commandment. Thus, prayer in Judaism can be a voluntary offering—just as some of the sacrifices in the old Temple cult were not a matter of legal requirements, but the free-will outpouring of human generosity. On the other hand, there are some prayers which are considered to be the fulfillment of an obligation which man has towards God—just as some of the

17

ancient sacrifices were mandatory, and not voluntary aspects of the cult.

Now, the concept of prayers which are "commanded" is not exactly an easy concept for the modern Jew to accept; and we shall revert to that problem later on. First of all, however, we must clarify the concept itself as it was traditionally understood. For you may search the Bible from the beginning to the end, assuming that the Bible is the record of God's commandments to Israel, and you will not find a single commandment which says: "Thou shalt pray!" What you will find, however, is a verse, Deuteronomy 11:13, which tells Israel "to love the Lord your God, and to serve Him with all your heart and with all your soul."

The Hebrew word in this verse, which is translated as "to serve" (ule'ovdo), is a word which, at one time, was primarily used in connection with the sacrificial cult. The Rabbis of the Talmud, therefore, asked about this verse: "What kind of service (avodah) is that which takes place in the heart?" And they answered their own question by saying:"It is prayer!"[1] In other words, when the Torah commands us to serve the Lord with all our heart, it is really commanding us to to pray. Thus prayer came to be regarded as a divine commandment, an obligation, a mitzvah.

Nevertheless, by thus construing the Bible verse about serving the Lord with all one's heart, the Rabbis did not mean to imply that the "commandment to pray" extends to all the prayers now found in the prayer book, which came into existence at a much later time. Indeed, as Maimonides, in the twelfth century, quite explicitly stated in commenting on the Rabbinic interpretation of "the service which takes place in the heart": "the number of prayers is not biblically commanded; and the wording of the prayer is not biblically commanded; and, according to the Torah, there is no fixed time for prayer."[2]

According to Maimonides, the biblical commandment to pray is to be construed as follows:—

A man should entreat God and pray every day, and proclaim the praise of the Holy One, praised be He. Afterwards he should voice his needs in petitionary prayer. And, after that, give praise and thanksgiving to God for the goodness which He has abundantly bestowed upon him. Everybody does so in accordance with his own ability. If, however, he was inhibited in speech, he would merely speak according to his ability and whenever he desired to do so. Similarly, the number of prayers would depend upon the ability of every individual. Some would pray but once every day, while others would pray many times.[3]

Maimonides then goes on to say that this situation obtained from the days of Moses (when the "commandment to pray" was first given) down to the days of Ezra, in the fifth century B.C.E. That is to say, using the categories of our previous chapter, while it was a biblical commandment to pray, the prayer intended by the Bible was only the prayer of *kavvanah*. The *keva* element had not yet come into the picture. However, prior to the days of Ezra, there was the Babylonian Exile, and it was during the Babylonian Exile that people experienced difficulties in praying. At that time, people's grasp of the Hebrew language proved to be insufficient to voice their needs, and they employed an odd jargon—a mixture of Hebrew and foreign languages—to address God in prayer. When Ezra and his law court saw that situation, "they arose and ordained for the people eighteen benedictions to be recited in sequence—the first three benedictions to consist of praise addressed to God, and the last three of thanksgiving, while the intermediate benedictions were to consist of petitions for various things, such as the main categories of all of man's desires and the community's needs."[4] They also ordained that the number of times that the prayer of the Eighteen Benedictions was to be recited was to correspond to the number of statutory sacrifices offered at the Jerusalem Temple.[5]

More recent scholarship does not agree with Maimonides in setting such an early date for the prayer of the Eighteen Benedictions as we know it.[6] But that is immaterial to our present concern. What matters to us here is that, according to Maimonides, the only prayer which is "commanded" is the Prayer of the Eighteen Benedictions. That, it should be clearly understood, was said in reference to the "commandment to *pray*." There are other parts of the liturgy the recitation of which is deemed to be a commandment—and not only a "Rabbinical" commandment (like praying the Eighteen Benedictions), but a commandment of the Bible itself. Many Jews today, finding those parts in the printed prayer book, may regard them as "prayers." But, to the ancient Rabbis, they were not a matter of "prayer," but of "declaration" or "proclamation."

We are referring to that rubric of the daily morning and evening service which is called, "The Recitation of the *Shema* and its Benedictions." The *Shema* itself consists of the following biblical passages: Deuteronomy 6:49; Deuteronomy 11:13-21; and Numbers 15:37-41. The obligation to recite those passages twice every day was derived from the text of the first paragraph of the *Shema* itself, where we read that "thou shalt speak (of these words) . . . when thou liest down, and when thou risest up."[7] But the Rabbis, who saw in those passages The Acceptance of the Yoke of God's Kingdom, The Acceptance of the Yoke of the Commandments, and (the Mention of) the Exodus from Egypt, respectively, also envisaged the recitation of the *Shema* to be embedded in a framework of benedictions which spell out the great Jewish affirmations of Creation, Revelation, and Redemption. Therefore, when the Rabbis spoke of the recitation of the *Shema* evening and morning, they meant not only the biblical passages we have listed above, but also the surrounding benedictions.[8]

The biblical commandment to *recite* the *Shema* and the Rabbinical commandment to *pray* the prayer of the Eighteen Benedictions were, therefore, in origin, two entirely different matters, as far as the Rabbis were concerned. However, in the course of time, efforts were made to join the prayer to the recitation.[9] At any rate, it is those two segments of the daily liturgy, the recitation and the prayer, which are regarded as the obligatory, the *chovah* part of Jewish prayer.

We thus come back to our initial statement that, in addition to the limitless times a Jew may pray when he feels so moved, there are also prayers which he is *obligated* to say. In terms of the problem which faces the modern Jew, it is relatively unimportant whether that which he is obligated to say consists of much or of little material. The difficulty lies in the concept itself, in the very idea that prayer is not just an emotional outlet, but a downright *obligation*. The sparse attendance at so many synagogue services in our day would seem to indicate that the concept of prayer as an obligation has largely lost its hold upon the modern Jew.

Such a concept was more acceptable to the Jew who saw specific divine imperatives behind every single tradition governing Jewish life—from the rules of diet to the prohibitions of the Sabbath law, and from the giving of charity to the selecting of the material for one's suit. Within such a total system of observance based on "commandments," and it is a system to which Orthodox Judaism still adheres, the *obligation* to pray could find its self-evident place. But what of the Jew who no longer believes in any doctrine of verbal inspiration, and who asks of any given observance that more can be said in its favor than the mere fact that "it is written" in the legal codes of old? Is there any way in which such a Jew can again make his own the concept of prayer as an obligation?

It would seem that there is. And it is again Maimonides who can serve as our guide. Consider, for example, what Maimonides has to say about the inclusion of the prayer of the Eighteen Benedictions in the evening service. It must be borne in mind that there was no unanimity among the Rabbis of the Talmud about the obligatory character of the evening prayer, primarily because there was no corresponding sacrifice in the Jerusalem Temple. Indeed, during the greater part of the Rabbinic period, it was held to have been a *voluntary* act of worship, and, for a long time, it was not made a part of the statutory evening devotion.[10] The fact that, to this very day, the Eighteen Benedictions are recited silently

only, and are not repeated aloud by the prayer leader in the
Orthodox and Conservative evening services, shows that in
the evening, the Eighteen Benedictions were never accorded
their full recognition as an "obligatory" prayer. However, in
the course of time, praying the Eighteen Benedictions in the
evening did become universal Jewish practice. And as
Maimonides says:

The Prayer of the evening is not an obligation. Nevertheless, in all of their
habitations, the Israelites have become accustomed to pray the evening
Prayer. They have, therefore, accepted it upon themselves *as though it were
an obligatory prayer.*[11]

The words, "as though it were an obligatory prayer," are, of
course, meant by Maimonides to refer to the Eighteen
Benedictions of the evening service only. Maimonides is very
careful in his use of words. For him, as we have seen, specific
prayers (as distinct from the general duty to worship God) are
only a Rabbinic, not a biblical ordinance. And the evening
Eighteen Benedictions are not even that. However, because
the Jewish people, wherever they dwell, have—volun-
tarily—made it a practice to pray the Eighteen Benedictions
in the evening, that practice is now to be regarded as though
it were on the same level of obligation as those other prayers
for which a higher degree of authority is invoked. In other
words, time-honored and universal Jewish practice is, in
itself, a source of obligation—even in instances where the
purely human origin of a given practice is clearly recognized
and admitted, and where no claim of a direct divine revelation
is being made.

This approach could well serve as a paradigm for the view
which the modernist Jew might take of the whole idea of
"commanded prayer." Admittedly, we are here going far
beyond the Maimonidean distinctions. Thus, even without
assuming that God thundered down from Mount Sinai the
commandment that man pray, and without necessarily
feeling bound by the specific manner in which the ancient
Rabbis construed such a purported commandment, the
modernist Jew could still relate to the prayer tradition of his

people "as though it were obligatory." He might do so because he is sufficiently impressed by the devotion which the Jewish people has lavished, everywhere and at all times, on the very minutiae of worship. There can, after all, be no doubt that the discipline of common prayer has contributed in no small measure to the very survival of the Jews as a cohesive group. There should, therefore, be no difficulty in understanding those practices which have made for the survival of Judaism and the cohesion of Jews as *mitzvot,* as obligations to be accepted by anyone who himself sees value in that survival and cohesion.

Yet the boon of "commanded prayer" is by no means exhausted by what it does for the Jews as a *people.* The individual, as an individual with spiritual potential, stands to gain as well. The ability to pray with which we have been endowed is an ability which we can develop further by actually engaging in the act of prayer on a regular basis. But it is also an ability which may atrophy because we do not sufficiently make use of it. In this respect, it is like most other abilities.

A writer, whether he feels like it or not, may on occasion force himself to abide by the ancient rule, *nulla dies sine linea,* not to let a single day pass without writing at least one line,[12] for he knows that the lack of practice will make it so much harder for him to write even if, on some future occasion, he may again "feel like" writing. Much the same can be said about the athlete who has to keep in shape, and about the musician who has to maintain his mastery of his chosen instrument. And just as the writer, and the athlete, and the musician may not always be "in the mood" to practise their skills, so the Jew may not always be "in the mood" to pray. Yet, if the Jew were to make his praying entirely dependent upon his moods, he may find soon enough that he has lost the ability to pray, to be on intimate terms with the Sovereign of the Universe—even if, one day, circumstances should produce the "mood" in which prayer is felt to be desirable. Prayer as an "obligation" keeps alive our ability to pray.

In his book, *Man's Quest for God,* Professor Abraham

Joshua Heschel describes his spiritual anguish while studying at the University of Berlin after having spent his
childhood in the pietistic environment of Eastern Europe. A
new and different world was opened up to him here. One
evening, as he was walking through the streets of Berlin, it
suddenly struck him that the sun had gone down, that
evening had arrived. But sunset, in the Jewish tradition, is
associated with the recitation of the evening *Shema;* and
young Heschel began to utter the words of the benedictions
preceding the evening *Shema.* Uttering those words, he began
to find himself again as a Jew, as a human being in God's
world. It was the "duty to worship" which reminded his
distraught mind that it was time to think of God. He would
not have done so otherwise. And Heschel confesses:

I am not always in a mood to pray. I do not always have the vision and the
strength to say a word in the presence of God. But when I am weak, it is the
law that gives me strength; when my vision is dim, it is duty that gives me
insight.[13]

Jewish worship today has, in many instances, been turned
into a means to satisfy the Jew's emotional needs, to respond
to his passing moods, and to bolster his ephemeral political
preferences. That is why so many "gimmicks" are in use to
"drum up" synagogue attendance—for the emotional needs,
the passing moods, and the political preferences never remain
the same for very long. Besides, there are so many other and
competing agencies which promise to take care of those very
moods and needs; and the synagogues fall all over themselves
trying to compete.

It may well be that, here and there, those synagogues have
been able to salvage something of the element of genuine
kavvanah, and to afford the individual an opportunity of
voluntary prayer. But there can be a real "service of the
heart" only when that service is truly a *service,* that is, a
service rendered to God by the man who feels *obligated* to
render such a service. The rediscovery of this obligation, and
perhaps it alone, is surely the key to the synagogue's survival.

Rabbi Eliezer Berkovits has described that relationship of

voluntary to obligatory prayer with fine insight:

When a man, overwhelmed by the impact of a specific experience, seeks the nearness of God or bursts forth in halleluyah or bows down in gratitude, it is prayer but not service of God yet; it is a human response to a potent stimulus. But when he prays without the stimulus of a specific occasion, acknowledging that man is always dependent on God, that independently of all personal experience God is always to be praised and to be thanked, then—and only then—is prayer divine service of the heart.[14]

Chapter Three

CULT, ENTERTAINMENT AND WORSHIP

Not all the "gimmicks" of the modern synagogues to "drum up" attendance necessarily merit indiscriminate condemnation. If, in many modern synagogues, attempts are being made to add "relevance" to the worship services and to make them more "entertaining," such attempts are not altogether without precedent in the liturgical tradition of Judaism. The question is not whether "relevant" and "entertaining" elements can be accommodated within the Jewish worship service, but rather whether a particular form of "entertainment" is appropriate to the place and to the occasion, and whether its absorption into the liturgical structure can be accomplished without doing violence to the structure as a whole.

In the evolution of Jewish prayer, we not only find, in the ongoing dialectics between *keva* and *kavvanah*, the constant intrusion of "relevance," but we also see that the element of "relevance" *(kavvanah)* quite often clothed itself in artistic (and, therefore, "entertaining") forms. In the course of its development, the synagogue service became ever more elaborate. It also became increasingly artistic, as synagogal poetry gained in complexity and sophistication.[1]

One of the most outstanding synagogal poets, Eleazar Kallir (6th/7th century?), whose poetry dominates the festival liturgy of German and Polish Jews, leaves us in no doubt that he is engaged in more than just straightforward praying. The meaning of a Kallirian poem is often quite puzzling. Understanding a stanza by Kallir requires not only a thorough knowledge of Bible and Rabbinic literature, but also a considerable intellectual effort. Grasping what the poet is trying to tell us is, to put it bluntly, a game. Some enjoy playing that game; others do not. And those others include an impressive array of authorities—from Abraham Ibn Ezra[2] to the founders of modern Reform Judaism.

But it is not only the hostile critic who regards Kallir's synagogal poetry as a "game." Kallir did so himself! In the opening line of his Prayer for Dew in the Additional Service of the first day of Passover, Kallir says:

> beda'to abi'ah chidot, be'am zu bezo lehachadot.
> With His approval, I shall utter riddles (!)
> To make happy this people (Israel) by this prayer for dew.

Kallir, then, openly admitted that he was providing entertainment in the form of riddles, an intellectual game, and that the purpose of his doing so was lehachadot, to make people happy.

Playing intellectual games involves one aspect of our personality. Enjoying music involves another. And music is an inseparable part of the Jewish worship service—whether we think of the melismatic trills of the prima donna cantor in a traditional synagogue or of Bloch's Sacred Service performed, with full orchestra, in a Reform temple. The music is there for the entertainment of the worshipper, rather than as a requirement of the Deity. True, the pious singer may hope that God will receive his songs with favor; he may, as the ancient psalmist did, call on his fellow-worshippers to praise God "with the blast of the horn, with the psaltery and harp, with the timbrel and dance, with stringed instruments and the pipe, with the loud-clanging cymbals, and with the clanging cymbals."[3] But the God who has been known to prefer justice to the sacrificial cult has also intimated His occasional distaste for musical performances. "Take thou away from Me the noise of thy songs;/ And let Me not hear the melody of thy psalteries" (Amos 5:23). Amos might be expected to have meant "psalteries" in a "broad sense," including even the pipe organ and the electric guitar.

However, Amos did so within a context where, in the absence of religious living outside of the sanctuary, the people concentrated their entire religious devotion on the pomp and splendor of the cult. The fact remains that the approved forms of Jewish worship, both biblical and Rabbinical, certainly do not rule out the pleasures of the senses. Quite the contrary! Voice, ear, nose, eye, palate and hand, all of them, in one way or another, are involved in the performance of the religious rites of Judaism. All of them participate in the Jew's acting out his devotion to God. There can be no doubt that Judah Halevi (ca. 1080/1140) was voicing sound Jewish doctrine when he said:

The divine law imposes no asceticism on us. Rather does it desire that we keep the balance and grant every mental and physical faculty its due, without overburdening one faculty at the expense of the other. Your contrition on a fast day brings you no nearer to God than your joy on the Sabbath and festivals.[4]

With the senses and enjoyment thus brought into the picture, the connection between worship and aesthetics becomes obvious. Worship must be beautiful! It would be tempting in this connection to quote as our proof text: "Worship the Lord in the beauty of holiness." [5] Alas, there is no such verse in the Hebrew Bible. The verse seems to be an invention of the translators employed by King James, who thus rendered *hishtachavu ladonai behadrat kodesh.* More recent translators and commentators are more or less in agreement in understanding *hadrat kodesh* as "holy array," i.e., the special garments appropriate to worship.[6] "The beauty of holiness" is a lovely phrase. But it is perhaps a little bit too abstract for the Jerusalem bard, and somewhat more appropriate to the mind of Hellas.

Yet what we may lack in abstraction, the Tradition provides concretely. Thus, in a comment on "Honour the Lord with thy substance" (Proverbs 3: 9), the *Midrash* explains:

If you have a pleasant voice, lead the congregation in the recitation of the *Shema* and in the Eighteen Benedictions. Chiyya bar Adda, the son of Bar Kappara's sister, had a pleasant voice. Bar Kappara would say to him: "My son, lead the congregation in the recitation of the *Shema* and in the Eighteen Benedictions, to fulfil the verse, 'Honour the Lord with thy substance,'—with that which He has graciously granted you."[7]

In the same vein we have Rabbi Ishmael's comment on the verse, "This is my God, and I will glorify Him" (Exodus 15: 2).

The word, *ve-anvehu,* commonly translated as "and I will glorify Him," could also be translated as "and I will *beautify* Him." This leads Rabbi Ishmael to ask: "But is it possible for a mere creature of flesh and blood to beautify his Creator?!" And he answers his own question by saying:

I shall be beautiful before Him in the performance of the commandments. I shall prepare before Him a beautiful *lulav,* a beautiful *sukkah,* beautiful *tzitzit,* and a beautiful phylactery.[8]

Note what is involved here. A Jew could fulfill the letter of the law by having a *sukkah* which is not quite so nice, or with a somewhat faded *lulav.* The minimum requirements are spelled out in the legal sources. But, over and above the strictly legal requirements, there are the aesthetic demands. The performance of a *mitzvah* must be beautiful! Beautiful, of course, by *man's* standards of beauty. What other standards of beauty does man have? Yet man's employment of beauty in the performance of a religious act itself assumes a religious dimension. Man becomes beautiful *before God.* Man's aesthetic enjoyment becomes part of the act of worship.

This, of course, is the Jewish concept of *hiddur mitzvah,* of adorning or beautifying the religious act.[9] *Hiddur mitzvah* is man's aesthetic way of living the life of *halakhah* (Jewish Law). On occasion, the aesthetic dimension might go far beyond what the *halakhah* is commonly understood to legislate. For example, the classical sources of Rabbinic Judaism are quite determined and specific when it comes to outlawing the imitation of non-Jewish religious observances, *chukkot hagoyim.*[10] And yet, we know that any number of details of the cult of the Second Temple were modeled on the generally prevailing practices of the Hellenistic world. But, as Professor Saul Lieberman explains, "in matters of external decorum the Jews might imitate the Gentiles without any feeling that they are breaking the law; after all, it was commendable 'to adorn a religious act.' "[11]

In general, however, we may be sure that aesthetic considerations were not allowed to override specific halakhic requirements. Aesthetics is what man *adds* to the halakhah;

but the halakhah itself must not be obliterated in the process. It has, as it were, a beauty of its own, the beauty of obedience, which remains primary. Thus, the great nineteenth-century legal expert, Moses Sopher, is absolutely explicit in making a distinction between the requirements of the Torah and the aesthetic additions made by man; and he places the latter very much in a secondary category. Speaking about the halakhic requirement that the *lulav* be tied together "with its own kind" (and not with any other kind of material), Moses Sopher says:

Not that is the required "beauty" which men invent by way of beautifications and adornments (of the *lulav*), but the beauty of the Torah. Therefore a man must first tie the *lulav* together with its own kind. Only after one has complied with the beauty demanded by the Torah is one able to beautify the *lulav* with golden rings, for the sake of endearing the commandment.[12]

It should be clear that, while there is scope for aesthetics, enjoyment and even entertainment in the act of Jewish worship, it is not *any* kind of enjoyment or entertainment, indiscriminately chosen, for which Jewish worship offers scope. There are, after all, certain rules which govern the whole enterprise—rules which address themselves to the propriety of the forms of entertainment selected, and rules which ensure that the whole act will be recognized for what it purports to be: an act of Jewish worship.

This holds true even if we leave the realm of the halakhah of liturgy and the theology of worship, and join the anthropologists in regarding the worship service as a "game" which people play. Says J. Huizinga:

The arena, the card-table, the magic circle, the temple, the stage, the screen, the tennis court, the court of justice, etc., are all in form and function play-grounds, i.e., forbidden spots, isolated, hedged around, hallowed, within which special rules obtain.[13]

And he continues to inform us that "all play has its rules. They determine what 'holds' in the temporary world circumscribed by play. The rules of the game are absolutely binding and allow no doubt."[14]

But can the theologian really accept the anthropologist's description of liturgy as a "game"? The late Romano Guardini answers this question emphatically in the affirmative. Noting that, "in a precise sense, it is impossible for liturgy to have a practical 'purpose,' for the simple reason that, as a matter of fact, it does not exist for the sake of man, but for the sake of God,"[15] Guardini says:

To play before God, to *be*, not to create a work of art, that is the innermost essence of liturgy. That is why we have the exalted mixture of profound seriousness and divine happiness in it. Only he who is able to take art and play seriously can understand why liturgy so carefully prescribes in a thousand regulations the nature of the words, the movements, the colors, and the vessels.[16]

Romano Guardini was a Roman Catholic, speaking about the liturgy of his Church. Can the same really be said also about the *Jewish* liturgy? Friedrich Heiler reminds us that "we can only . . . speak inexactly of a synagogal . . . *liturgy*, for 'liturgy' according to the sense of the word is a holy, sacramental act which brings the believer into a sensuous yet spiritual communion with the divine."[17] And Heiler insists that, "whilst the mystery stands as the central feature of primitive Christian and Catholic worship, it is completely absent from the worship of Mohammedans and Jews."[18]

There is something in the modern Jewish make-up which will induce many Jewish modernists to respond with a hearty "Amen" to Heiler's description. No mystery cults for them! Theirs is a "prophetic" kind of worship! Confidently they refer to Maimonides' sober observation that, while it is indeed a biblical commandment to pray every day, the number of prayers and the prayer formulae themselves were not biblically commanded.[19] That, of course, is something quite different from the thought of a divinely instituted sacrament with which a Catholic invests his concept of "liturgy"!

Yet there is another side to that story as well. The details of the prayer service, as Maimonides rightly insists, were not ordained in the Torah. But the Torah does state quite elaborately the details of the sacrificial cult. And the prayers of the synagogue are not altogether unrelated to the

sacrificial cult of the Temple—however much some modernist
Jews would like to play off the one against the other. As
Evelyn Underhill reminds us:

Both Temple and Synagogue were accepted as the two aspects of one total
response to God. . . They were parts of a single worshipping life, in which
outward and inward, provincial and national devotion, were directed to one
end—two ways of expressing one love—and there was from the beginning a
close organic connection between them.[20]

The traditional liturgy of the synagogue tends to substanti-
ate Miss Underhill's observation—not only by its constantly
reiterated petitions for the rebuilding of the Temple, but also,
and above all, by those numerous biblical and Rabbinic
passages, dealing with the minutiae of the sacrificial cult,
which have been incorporated into the traditional prayerbook. This was done because the synagogal prayer service was
regarded as a substitute for the sacrificial cult. In the words
of Rabbi Joshua ben Levi, "the statutory services of the
synagogue have been ordained to correspond to the daily
Temple offerings."[21]

That view was still taken seriously by some of the
nineteenth-century Reformers. One of them, Abraham Adler,
even went so far as to disagree with a well-known view of
Maimonides which most other Reform Jewish thinkers have
always delighted to quote: that the sacrificial legislation was
merely a "concession" which God made to biblical Israel.[22]

Said Abraham Adler in 1845:

The view of Maimonides, according to which the sacrificial cult was only an
accommodation to the paganism from which the people could not altogether
free itself . . . is undoubtedly an erroneous one. How else could we account
for the fact that the sacrificial laws were laid down to the last
minutia? . . . The idea then created for itself a new and more appropriate
form, that of prayer. In that sense we must understand the talmudic
passage, "They ordained the prayers to correspond to the daily sacrifices."
We cannot, therefore, become indifferent to the sacrificial cult.[23]

"Prayer—a substitute for sacrifice!" This has become an
empty slogan for many who mouth that phrase. But Adler
really meant it. Because he meant it, prayer, for him,
assumed something of the demanding quality as well as of the

mystical devotion which the ancient sacrificial cult had enjoyed. There was to be something as permanent and as "set" about the prayer service of the synagogue as there had been about the continual offering (tamid) of old. And it was another radical Reform leader, David Einhorn, who chose the name, Olat Tamid ("a continual burnt-offering") for his Reform prayer book, published in 1856. The words of Numbers 28:6, "A continual burnt-offering, as ordained on Mount Sinai for a sweet savor, an offering made by fire to the Lord," are programmatically inscribed on the title page of Einhorn's ritual.

It is almost superfluous to add that neither Adler nor Einhorn anticipated or wished for the ultimate restoration of the sacrificial cult. For them, it was definitely an outgrown form of religious devotion. But, behind the form, which is temporal, there is the idea, which is eternal; and it is the idea behind the sacrificial cult which today manifests itself in Jewish prayer.

As Guardini put it in a different context:

Anyone who takes his relationship to God seriously soon sees that prayer is not merely an expression of the inner life which will prevail on its own, but is also a service to be performed in faith and obedience.[24]

There is nothing in those words with which Judaism could disagree. When all is said and done, the same Maimonides, who tells us that there are no biblically prescribed prayer formulae, also bequeathed to us his Laws (!) of Prayer and his Laws (!) of Benedictions.

The modern synagogue stands in succession to the ancient Temple. That is why the modern synagogue, in addition to all of its other functions, must provide the modern Jew with the kind of spiritual and religious outlet which his ancestors found in the Jerusalem shrine. And that includes, in addition to legitimate "entertainment" and social "relevance," a service "to be performed in faith and obedience," an opportunity of fulfilling the mitzvah of prayer, and a liturgical framework which possesses something of the permanence of the old continual burnt-offerings.

Thus we have come back to the concept of "liturgy," a concept to which, as we have seen, we may be more entitled than Friedrich Heiler seemed to think. Liturgy, however, as Guardini recognized, can be taken seriously only by those who take art and play seriously. For liturgy is a "game" which, like all other games, according to Huizinga, has its rules—rules which "are absolutely binding and allow no doubt."

To create within the boundary of those rules, that would be the true work of art to be wrought by modern Jewish liturgical endeavors. The challenge which we face is one of fashioning the ingredients of both cult and entertainment, tradition and relevance, into a unified and integrated whole, which spells: Worship.

Chapter Four
PETITION AND PRAISE

The prayer of petition, the request for something addressed to God, is both the most natural form of prayer which man utters and, at the same time, the most difficult form of prayer to justify theologically. The most natural form of prayer; for what can be more natural than for man to ask for what he needs, to request what he wants, and to plead for what he desires? The petitionary prayers in the Jewish liturgy include petitions for material goods as well as for spiritual blessings, for physical healing as well as for messianic redemption, for the destruction of arrogance as well as for the granting of peace, and for intelligence as well as for divine pardon. There is no legitimate human concern which remains outside the scope of Jewish petitionary prayer.

Yet the God to whom such petitionary prayers are addressed is, by definition, an all-knowing God. He would not be God if He had to be told by man what man needs. How, then, can petitionary prayer be justified theologically?

Now, it is quite clear that the very Rabbis who instituted the prayer of the Eighteen Benedictions, the petitionary prayer *par excellence,* firmly believed in a God who did not have to be told about man's needs. This becomes obvious when we consider the kind of prayer which they devised for emergency situations, i.e., for moments of danger and crisis when man is unable to concentrate on the full Eighteen Benedictions. Here are some of them:—

According to Rabbi Joshua, the following prayer should be said:

Save, O Lord, Thy people, the remnant of Israel. In every time of crisis let their needs be before Thee. Praised art Thou, O Lord, who hearest prayer.[1]

According to Rabbi Eliezer, one should pray as follows:

35

Do Thy will in heaven above, and grant equanimity to those who fear Thee below, and do that which is good in Thine eyes. Praised art Thou, O Lord, who hearest prayer.[2]

Others, again, prefer this prayer:

The needs of Thy people Israel are many, and their understanding is limited. May it be Thy will, O Lord our God, to give to each one his sustenance and to each body what it lacks. Praised art Thou, O Lord, who hearest prayer.[3]

Somewhere between the emergency situations presupposed by the prayers just quoted and the requisite leisure for the recitation of the full Eighteen Benedictions, there is the abbreviated form of the Eighteen Benedictions meant for wayfarers and workers during working hours. It has the first three and the last three regular benedictions; but all the intermediate benedictions are contracted into a single one, which concludes with "Praised art Thou, O Lord, who hearest prayer." But immediately preceding this conclusion, we find the words, based on Isaiah 65:24, "Before we call, Thou wilt answer."[4]

What all those substitute prayers for the Eighteen Benedictions have in common, and what they all explicitly state, is the conviction that God does not need to be told, that He is fully aware of our needs, and that, even before we utter our needs, God is ready to respond. And Rabbi Eliezer's prayer, "Do that which is good in Thine eyes," is really all that has to be said, calling to mind Rabban Gamaliel's advice: "Make His will as your will."[5]

There can, then, be no doubt about the exalted views of God and of prayer held by the ancient Rabbis. Perhaps we would even have been able to understand it if those Rabbis, who assigned such highly sophisticated prayers to "emergency" situations—that is to say, to situations when man really feels impelled to cry out to God—had not bothered at all about petitionary prayers for more leisurely moments. Suppose they had said to us: "Such-and-such are the formulae to be used when you are in dire straits. Apart from that, your prayers to God should be strictly prayers of adoration and thanksgiving.

God knows your needs before you utter them. So, do not blaspheme by listing your wants!" Given the Rabbis' belief in an all-knowing God, they *could* quite easily have said something like that. But that is precisely what they did *not* say. On the contrary, particularly for those times when we are not in distress, they provided us with the formulae of petitionary prayer, and insisted that those formulae be regularly recited!

Since, therefore, the petitionary prayers could not have been meant for the purpose of conveying information to God, it would follow that they have been devised for the benefit of *man*. It is as though the Rabbis were telling us: "Even though God does not have to be told about your needs, He has given you an opportunity of opening your heart to Him, of sharing your concerns with Him. Petitionary prayer does not convey any information to God, which He previously lacked, but it affords you the relief of verbalizing, in His presence, whatever it is that you are striving for."

Basically, there are three main advantages in availing ourselves of the petitionary prayers furnished by the Tradition:—

(a) There is, first of all, the recognition of our dependence upon God. We are not alone in the world. Our limited human strength is not the only power which gets things accomplished. With the help of God, goals can be reached which would otherwise be beyond us. Petitionary prayer makes us aware of this.

(b) Petitionary prayer, sanctioned by Tradition, also gives us the confidence that what we are asking for is in consonance with the teachings of our religion. We do not pray for the attainment of goals which would be contrary to the aims of our faith or irreconcilable with the nature of God as Judaism conceives of Him. Consequently, knowing that what we express in prayer is acceptable to God, we can feel all the more assured of divine help in the attainment of our verbalized goals.

(c) Petitionary prayer, sanctioned by Tradition, enlarges the range of our concerns. People can become very egotistical and self-centered in prayer. They can confine their prayers to their own very immediate concerns, paying little attention, if any, to the needs and the concerns of their fellowmen. But a petitionary prayer, uttered by a whole community, can save us from such pitfalls.

A curious report is contained in the Palestinian Talmud about the prayers which the High Priest recited in the Jerusalem Temple on the Day of Atonement. In addition to praying for the material and the spiritual blessings to be enjoyed by Israel in the new year, the High Priest also asked God to pay no attention to the prayer of the wayfarers![6] Here was the highest religious functionary of the Jewish people, asking God to pay no attention to the prayer of one segment of the population! Of course, God no more has to be told what *not* to do than He has to be informed about the actions He is desired to take. The curious request of the High Priest was merely a dramatic way of expressing disapproval of a certain type of prayer. But what was it that the wayfarers asked God to do? Quite simply, to withhold the rain! If you travel on the open road, rain can be a terrible nuisance, and the traveler would rather have good weather for his journey. And so he would pray to God for good weather. Such a prayer looks innocent enough—until we begin to realize that the prayer was uttered in an agricultural society which depended for its very survival upon the timely fall of rain. Indeed, the High Priest specifically prayed for such a timely rainfall and, in that prayer, he voiced the concern of the people as a whole. The wayfarers, on the other hand, dissociated themselves from that overriding national concern, unable to look beyond their immediate private interest. The High Priest, for his part, expressed the conviction that the common good should come before the sectional interests. The fact that this difference of opinion was expressed liturgically makes it relevant to our present consideration.

The petitions contained within the Eighteen Benedictions have always made the Jew aware of the needs of the whole Jewish people. By rehearsing those needs he identified himself with his people, and he was taught to think not only in terms of his individual needs, but also in terms of the needs of all Israel. It was, therefore, spiritually shortsighted when, in the nineteenth century, the Reformers in Western Europe and in America felt free to abolish some of the traditional petitions simply because *they* no longer felt the need to have those petitions granted *for themselves.* There was, of course, no reason for nineteenth-century American Jewry to implore God to "look upon our afflictions . . . and redeem us speedily." But there were millions of fellow-Jews in Eastern Europe who were still very much in need of speedy redemption. And who can gauge the lack of commitment to a common past and a common destiny which was implicit in the refusal to pray for the rebuilding of Jerusalem! Of course, we can understand why, at the time, those prayers were omitted. But, then, we can also *understand* the prayer of the wayfarers. The point, however, is that, in the one case as in the other, individual and sectional interests were allowed to over-ride the concerns of the people as a whole. And that is precisely the kind of situation which the fixed traditional prayer of petition attempts to prevent.

It is in the nature of any discussion of petitionary prayer that the question arises whether God "answers" prayer. An unequivocally affirmative answer is given to this question both in the Bible and in Rabbinic literature. But just as unequivocal is the testimony of those who have prayed and have then found that their petitions have not been granted. It all depends on how one looks upon petitionary prayer and upon—God.

After all, it would be a rather primitive concept of God if one were to regard Him as a kind of cosmic vending machine. You insert a prayer, and out comes whatever boon you have selected! This is not to say that such concepts of God and of prayer have never been held within the confines of Judaism. But such popular notions of prayer do not represent Judaism's most mature thought on this subject.

The view which sees prayer as "answered" only when the specific good we have requested is actually granted is a view which leaves out of account the kind of sentiment voiced in

the "emergency prayers" which we have considered at the
beginning of this chapter. One of those prayers expressed the
thought that, while the needs of Israel were many, Israel's
understanding in formulating them was limited. Another
prayer, that of Rabbi Eliezer, asked God to do that which is
good in His own sight. Clearly, there is a recognition here of
the fact that, while God *is* concerned with man's highest good,
man's formulation of what he, man, *thinks* is his highest good
is not necessarily always adequate. Man, in fact, may voice
requests which, in the long run, are *not* for his own good. If
God were to grant such requests, then He would not really be
concerned with man's true welfare.

Put differently, the same thought may be expressed by
saying that God's "answer" to man's prayer need not
invariably be an affirmative answer. God must also be
thought capable of saying "No!" Perhaps this is indeed the
major difference between engaging in magic and engaging in
prayer. Magic, by definition, *must* work. If it does not yield
results, then, in the view of the practitioner of magic,
something must have gone wrong with the performance of the
magical rite; and he will repeat the rite in a more careful and
meticulous manner. Prayer, on the other hand, is addressed to
a God who has a will and a mind of His own. God cannot be
manipulated by man. He can only be *addressed.* He may, or
may not grant a specific request. But there is no mechanism
of man's devising which would compel Him to do so. In
addressing God, man knows that a "No" can be as much of an
"answer" as a "Yes."

Moreover, a divine "answer" is already implicit in man's
very capacity to pray. Here we have in mind man's capacity to
invest the words of the prayer with real personal meaning
and significance, and not just the ability to *read* the words
printed in the prayer book. My very ability to pray shows me
that I am "in tune" with the divine will, that I am assured of
divine help in my striving for the realization of the goals
formulated in my prayers. Perhaps that is the true meaning
of the Prophetic utterance:

And it shall come to pass that, before they call, I will answer, and while they are yet speaking, I will hear.[7]

There is, however, yet another aspect of Jewish petitionary prayer which deserves our special attention. Normally, the prayers of petition and the prayers of praise are distinct types of prayer. If we want something, we utter the prayer of petition. If we are grateful, we utter the prayer of praise. Yet it is the peculiar genius of Judaism that many of its petitionary prayers—and all of the petitionary prayers which have gone into the making of the Eighteen Benedictions— conclude on a note of praise. They are, therefore, as much prayers of praise as they are prayers of petition. And this, too, has its profound theological implications.

Consider, for example, the first petitionary prayer included in the Eighteen Benedictions. It is a prayer for knowledge and intelligence.

> O Thou, who favorest man with knowledge,
> and teachest mortals understanding,
> favor us with knowledge, understanding and discernment from Thee.
> Praised art Thou, O Lord, gracious Giver of knowledge.

Suppose, then, that I utter this prayer as a genuine request for greater knowledge and understanding. Suppose furthermore that, from one day to the next, or from one year to the next, I have not grown perceptibly in knowledge and understanding. Nevertheless, before I conclude that my prayer for knowledge has not been answered, I had better look around me a little. Chances are that I shall find some highly intelligent and understanding people, people, that is, who *have* been favored with knowledge, understanding and discernment by God. Though I personally may not yet be a direct beneficiary, the petitionary prayer for knowledge and understanding has indeed been "answered," and continues to be "answered" in the world at large every day. It is, therefore, quite appropriate for me to continue praising Him who is the gracious Giver of knowledge.

The same applies to all of the other petitions included in the Eighteen Benedictions. They are, in fact, *benedictions*, that is,

praises, as much as they are petitions. They praise God for
what He has done, for what He can do, and for what He will
do. And the recipients of God's "answer" are mentioned in the
plural, not in the singular. The individual thus learns to look
upon himself as a part of the whole faith-community of Israel.
The concerns and the woes of his people become his own woes
and concerns, even as the hopes and aspirations of the group
become those of the individual. In the process, the individual
Jew begins to see his own needs from a larger perspective—a
perspective which enables him, even in moments of personal
distress, to praise God as well as to petition Him, to thank as
well as to plead.

Petitionary prayer, as we have seen, is a human need
rather than something required by God. God knows our needs
before we utter them, and He will do what is good in His sight.
But man was afforded an opportunity of rehearsing his wants
and his concerns before God. It was the genius of Judaism to
turn man's petitionary prayer into a praise of God. Once we
understand this, we may also understand the daring
statement in the Talmud that "the Holy One, praised be He, is
longing for the petitionary prayers of the righteous."[8]

Chapter Five

HEBREW AND VERNACULAR PRAYER

Few items in the wide range of Jewish legal literature are spelled out as clearly and as unequivocally as the permission—if not, indeed, the mandate—to pray in the language which one understands, whether that language be the "Holy Tongue" (Hebrew) or any other language. Already the *Mishnah,* the earliest extant codification of Rabbinic law, lists "the *Shema,* the Prayer (of the Eighteen Benedictions), and the Grace after Meals" among the ritual and liturgical passages which "may be recited in any language."[1]

Maimonides, in his code of Rabbinic law, says:

All the benedictions *(berakhot)* may be said in any language, provided one says them according to their essential character, as ordained by the Sages. And, if one has deviated from the formula, as long as he has mentioned the Name of God and His Kingdom and the subject matter of the benediction, even in the vernacular, he has fulfilled his obligation.[2]

The thirteenth-century *Book of the Pious* states explicitly:

It is better for a man to say his Prayer (of the Eighteen Benedictions) and to recite the *Shema* and the benedictions in a language which he understands than for him to pray in the Holy Tongue if he does not understand it.[3]

Even the sixteenth-century *Shulchan Arukh,* the last great authoritative codification of Jewish law considered binding by Orthodox Judaism, leaves us in no doubt about the legitimacy of prayer in the vernacular:

A man can pray in whatever language he desires. This applies to prayer offered in a congregation. But an individual should pray only in the Holy Tongue. However, there are those who say that the latter provision applies only to him who voices his own needs, such as one who prays on behalf of a sick person or on account of some other suffering in his own household; but that, in the case of the prayer which is fixed for the whole congregation,

43

even the individual may recite it in any language. And there are those who say that even the individual voicing his own needs may do so in any language he desires, except in Aramaic.[4]

The exclusion of Aramaic from the languages suitable for prayer is based on a view in the Talmud to the effect that the ministering angels, who carry man's prayers to God's Throne of Glory, do not understand Aramaic.[5] It should be remembered, however, that no such consideration prevented the classical Jewish liturgists from composing the *Kaddish* and some other prayers in the Aramaic language! At any rate, it is quite clear that even the *Shulchan Arukh* sanctions prayer in the vernacular. The law is absolutely clear on that point.

When, however, the early Reformers of the nineteenth century—at first, to a rather limited extent—began to avail themselves of this provision of the law, and used the vernacular for portions of their worship services, the defenders of Tradition furiously attacked them as heretical innovators![6] It was a curious battle, for the law was so clearly on the side of the Reformers; and the Orthodox had to resort to all kinds of forays into numerology and mysticism in order to deny that the legal sources actually said what they blatantly seemed to be saying.

Yet, though perhaps not quite as "heretical" as the Orthodox thought them to have been, the early Reformers were indeed "innovators." Synagogal prayer in the vernacular, in the nineteenth century, *was* an innovation! Some two thousand years before, in the Hellenistic-Roman diaspora, synagogal prayer in the Greek vernacular was taken for granted. But that was a long time ago. The really amazing thing is that, ever since the *Mishnah* codified the permissibility of prayer in the vernacular, Jews, as a whole, simply made no use of that provision. Of course, here and there, an Aramaic prayer found its way into the worship service; vernacular translations of Scripture readings were customary in some localities during certain periods; some Arabic found its way into the Passover *seder* of a number of Oriental Jewish communites; and devotional manuals—primarily intended for women—were occasionally published in the vernacular or in Jewish dialects thereof. But no Jewish community until the nineteenth century, as far as we know, availed itself of the right to recite the *Shema* and to pray the Eighteen Benedictions in a language other than Hebrew. This goes for the Jews of the Rhineland as well as for the Jews of Andalusia, for the Jews of Poland as well as for the Jews of Italy, and for the Jews of China as well as for the Jews of Egypt.

No doubt, throughout the centuries, there have always been *some* Jews whose familiarity with the Hebrew language was such that they saw no need to avail themselves of the permission to pray in any other language. But it is hard to believe that, during a period of some eighteen hundred years, Hebrew was so *generally* known among the Jews that *all* of them would have regarded it as only natural to commune with God in that language. It seems more likely that the very opposite was the case, that such Hebrew knowledge as prevailed among the masses was imparted and acquired precisely because the service of the synagogue was in Hebrew, and people had to be trained to participate in it. Without a Hebrew worship service, it is extremely doubtful whether even a minimal knowledge of the bare mechanics of Hebrew reading would have survived the vicissitudes of diaspora existence outside of a rather limited scholarly class. By conducting their worship in Hebrew, the Jews, as it were, saved their erstwhile national language from total extinction.

And, in its turn, the Hebrew language as used in the synagogue service contributed to the cohesion of the far-flung Jewish communities. It was possible for a Jew from Regensburg to attend a synagogue service in Cairo, and to know what it was all about, and for an eighteenth-century Polish-Jewish movement like Hasidism to take over the liturgy of a sixteenth-century group of Palestinian mystics of mostly Spanish and Portuguese provenance. Thus, the great renunciation—as we might well call it—of the option of vernacular prayer, a renunciation which quite possibly implied the loss of a certain degree of meaningfulness in the very act of prayer, nevertheless redounded to the ultimate advantage of Judaism itself.

But thus far we have been dealing with almost *external* factors. That intelligibility in prayer is to be given up for the sake of Jewish cohesiveness and survival is, after all, a proposition which can be attacked (by the "spiritually-minded") just as easily as it can be defended (by the dedicated "survivalist"). There are, however, other considerations as well when it comes to prayer in Hebrew rather than in the vernacular; and they apply both to him whose knowledge of the Hebrew language barely extends beyond the mere mechanics of reading its consonants and vowels, and to him whose knowledge of the language has reached the point of mastery.

To take the second case first, let us bear in mind the genius of the Hebrew language which manages to convey a multitude of meanings in but a few well-chosen words. Each word comes with its own overtones and undertones, and numberless are the Bible verses which are open to more than one interpretation. There are, for example, the six opening words of the *Shema: Shema yisrael adonai elohenu adonai echad.* What do those words really *mean?* In his *Principles of the Jewish Faith,* Rabbi Louis Jacobs brings together a number of different English translations which have gained a certain currency—from "Hear, O Israel: The Lord our God is one Lord" (of the Authorized Version) to "Hear, O Israel! The Lord is our God, the Lord alone" (of the new version of the Jewish Publication Society). Jacobs follows this up by giving us no less than thirty (!) different interpretations of the identical six Hebrew words, ranging from the second century through the twentieth.[7]

Obviously, not all of those interpretations could possibly coincide with the original meaning of the *Shema;* yet any number of different interpretations are far from being mutually exclusive. The word *echad,* for example, does mean "one." (God is one, not many.) But it can also mean "unique" (God is unique, incomparable to anything else) as well as "alone" (the Lord alone is to be worshipped; the worship of anything else is prohibited idolatry). Now, the Hebraist reciting the *Shema* may, each time he recites the *Shema*, linger over this or that word, and meditate on the full range of its implications. Or he may have one meaning in mind today, and become conscious of another meaning tomorrow. The passage could mean something new to him each time he recites it and thinks about it.

But he who reads the *Shema* in a translation has cut himself off from the full range of meanings. Instead, he becomes dependent upon one man's or one committee's *interpretation*—that of the translator or the translators—to the virtual exclusion of all other possible interpretations. His recitation of the *Shema* in the vernacular may still be a proud affirmation of his monotheistic faith, but, unlike the Hebrew original, it is strictly one-dimensional.

Not everything in the Jewish prayer book is as amenable to so many different and legitimate interpretations as are the six opening words of the *Shema*. But, composed as they so largely are of biblical idiom and phraseology, most of the prayers in our prayer book carry a far wider meaning than the one meaning to which the translator into the vernacular has to confine himself. Here, again, the Hebraist who reads the same prayer time and time again, concentrating on different nuances and shades of meaning each time he reads it, is far less likely to find that prayer "boring" because of the constant repetition than the man who constantly repeats the vernacular translation of the identical prayer. For the Hebraist, prayer in Hebrew carries the promise of a far richer spiritual and intellectual experience than prayer in the vernacular could ever vouchsafe to him who is forever limited to the one interpretation perpetuated by the translator.

So much for the advantages accruing to the Hebrew scholar who prays in Hebrew. But what positive thing can be said about the Hebrew prayer of the Jew whose knowledge of the language hardly goes beyond a mechanical reading ability, and whose knowledge of the contents of the Hebrew prayers is of only the vaguest kind? It goes without saying that he does not enjoy any of the advantages we have mentioned in the case of the Hebraist. Quite the contrary. While the Hebraist sees more meaning in the Hebrew text than a vernacular translation could offer, the non-Hebraist, looking at the Hebrew text, may see no meaning at all! What he does see, however, is a "holy language," an accumulation of sounds which are not exactly "strange" (because, being Jewish, he has seen and heard Hebrew before; he knows that Hebrew is the language of the synagogue), but which are totally unrelated to the sounds of the marketplace, to the language of everyday living. It is a "special" language for a very "special" kind of communication. It carries the overtones of eternity, the intimations of a transcendent reality—just because its sounds do not translate themselves, for him, into any objective references to mundane existence.

That, perhaps, is one of the main reasons why, in the history of worship, the use of sacred languages, no longer understood by the worshippers, is not an unusual phenomenon. Friedrich Heiler has pointed out that

ancient and sacred formulas of prayer are still in use long after a complete change in religious conceptions—nay, the prayers continue to be recited even though their language has ceased to be understood. In the time of the Roman Empire old Latin prayers were still spoken which were completely unintelligible even to the priests. Sometimes such ancient formulas were transplanted even to countries where a foreign tongue was spoken.[8]

Even words in a language which is literally understood have to be invested with meaning by the worshipper before they can convey the burden of his heart as a *prayer*. Sometimes the worshipper succeeds in investing those words with meaning, or *kavvanah*, and sometimes he does not. On the other hand, there are occasions when the worshipper reaches the peak of the worship experience even though no words are being used at all. Such is the case when, in a traditional synagogue, the cantor engages in wordless—so-called melismatic—trills, during which many Jews, particularly those of East European provenance, experience the height of their devotion. Such, too, is the case when, to the sound of organ accompaniment, many a Reform Jew opens his heart in silent, and often wordless, prayer. In both cases, the worshipper uses the sounds he hears, i.e., the melismatic trills

of the cantor or the sound of the organ, as vehicles to carry his
innermost thoughts before the Holy One, praised be He.

In the light of this, it should not be too difficult to
understand how countless Jews, throughout the ages, have
used the sounds of the Hebrew prayers as vehicles for their
devotion, without being able to translate those prayers into
the vernacular. After all, they knew themselves to be in the
presence of God and in the company of their fellow-Jews.
Their hearts were full. They did not have to be told what to
pray for. And the Hebrew sounds, hallowed by an ancient
tradition, were known to be the accepted and acceptable form
of offering the prayer to God. When the heart is full, the
worshipper is not disturbed by a prayer language he does not
understand. (But, when the heart is empty, sitting through a
service which you do not understand can be a very taxing
experience—which would lead us to the conclusion that the
worshipper's heart may often be in greater need of reform
than the worshipper's language.)

We need not, however, rely on hypothesis. What has just
been said is being demonstrated time and again when
mourners make a point of reciting the *Kaddish* prayer—particularly those mourners who all too often are stumbling
through an English transliteration of the Aramaic-Hebrew
text. Now, while there is a form of the *Kaddish* which
specifically mentions the dead and their ultimate resurrection,[9] the recitation of that form of the *Kaddish* is confined to
the actual burial service (and to the celebration which marks
the conclusion of the study of a tractate of the Talmud). The
so-called *Mourners' Kaddish,* which is recited at the conclusion of all daily services, and which figures so largely during
the first eleven months after bereavement and thereafter on
the recurring anniversary of the death,[10] is a form of the
Kaddish which, in the traditional synagogue, makes no
mention of the dead at all!

What is called the *Mourners' Kaddish* is essentially a
doxology, that is, praises addressed to God, proclaiming God's
holiness and the hope for the establishment of His Kingdom.
Added to this are petitions for life and for peace. In its origin,

this prayer had nothing whatsoever to do with death and
bereavement. When—probably around the thirteenth
century[11]—it became customary for orphans to recite the
Kaddish at the conclusion of every service, the gesture
seemed to indicate, at first, that, though suffering a great
loss, the mourner nevertheless affirms before the assembled
congregation: "The Lord hath given, and the Lord hath taken
away; praised be the Name of the Lord" (Job 1: 21).

That, however, is certainly *not* what the *Kaddish* came to
mean among the Jewish masses. Embedded in legend and
folklore, and not totally bereft of superstitious elements, the
Kaddish gained in significance and importance to the degree
to which it was increasingly regarded as a prayer for the dead.
The recitation of the *Kaddish* was believed to be an effective
means of sparing the departed some of the presumed
sufferings in the Hereafter. It should be noted that the actual
wording of the *Kaddish* was not changed in the traditional
synagogue. The new meaning was, as it were, carried into the
words—regardless of what the words themselves literally
meant.

The same is, no doubt, true when secularly enlightened (but
Jewishly ignorant) modern Jews recite the *Kaddish* "for their
departed" today. It may be assumed that they do not believe
that the recitation of the *Kaddish* will actually affect the
welfare of souls in the Hereafter. But it may likewise be
assumed that the *Kaddish* is made the vehicle for the
expression of all kinds of feelings and emotions which the
survivor has for the deceased—none of them having anything
to do with the wording of the *Kaddish.*

Whatever, then, may be read *into* the *Kaddish,* be it
sublime or naive, the fact remains that the literal meaning of
the *Kaddish* words themselves bears little relation, if any, to
the function assigned to this prayer in the religious and
psychological life of him who recites it. On the contrary, one
might almost be tempted to assert that the significance of the
Kaddish as a "prayer for the dead" stands in an inverse ratio
to the knowledge of Hebrew and Aramaic on the part of the
man who so regards the *Kaddish.* The point, then, has been

made that the use of an unintelligible language need be no barrier to the prayer experience.

But another point has been made as well. Worship in a language one does not understand may be conducive to free association, and may serve as a stimulus for the outpouring of one's heart before God. But that is not all that Jewish prayer was meant to be. We have noted in our first chapter that long before the actual words of Jewish prayer became fixed, the ancient Rabbis laid down certain regulations about the ideas and the thoughts which ought to find expression in Jewish worship. They were also concerned with the *order* in which those thoughts and ideas were to be expressed. The Jewish prayer book is called *siddur* (literally, "order"), because the Jewish worship service was *not* conceived in terms of free association, but was meant to follow a certain sequence and order. Moreover, there are some thoughts and sentiments which should *not* find expression in a Jewish worship service, which are inappropriate or un-Jewish. (Some of us might feel that understanding the *Kaddish* as a "prayer for the dead" belongs in that category.) Yet if the worshipper is totally ignorant of the language in which worship is conducted, if he invests the unintelligible Hebrew sounds with any and all meanings which happen to come into his mind, something very harmful to the true Jewish worship experience may happen. It is in the light of such possible distortion of Jewish worship that we have to see the advice given by the *Book of the Pious:* "It is better for a man to say his Prayer (of the Eighteen Benedictions) and to recite the *Shema* and the benedictions in a language which he understands than for him to pray in the Holy Tongue if he does not understand it." Surely, whatever may be said in favor of Hebrew as the language of Jewish prayer, there are limits to the advantage of prayer in a language which one does not understand. And the great legal authorities of Judaism, whom we have quoted at the beginning of this chapter, were fully aware of those limits, and they gave their rulings accordingly.

What, then, was the great nineteenth-century controversy all about? Why was there this fierce Orthodox opposition to

prayer in the vernacular? Why could not the learned
defenders of Tradition see that the law in this respect was so
clearly on the side of the Reformers?

The answer, it would seem, lies in the *motivation* which
induced the early Reformers to espouse the cause of
vernacular prayer. In arguing for the legality of prayer in the
vernacular, the Reformers did not confine themselves to
pointing out that masses of Jews, particularly in the West,
were no longer conversant with Hebrew, and that, therefore,
for the benefit of those many Jews the synagogue service
should also contain prayers in the vernacular. Such an
argument, coupled, perhaps, with the institution of adult
Hebrew classes, might indeed have been irrefutable. But that
was not really what the Reformers were after. Hidden, and
perhaps not so hidden, behind the advocacy of prayer in the
vernacular, was the desire to revolutionize the very nature of
Judaism and the self-awareness of Jews.

As early as 1817, Eduard Kley, later to become a preacher
at the Hamburg Temple, had paid his respects to the Hebrew
language as the language in which the Torah was revealed
and as a "sweet echo from the days of childhood." Hebrew will
indeed remain holy and venerable "for everyone who still
reveres the past as an experienced mother, as a wise teacher
from whom he can always obtain advice." Yet Kley continued:

> But seven times more holy to us is the language which belongs to the
> present and to the soil whence we have sprung forth, . . . the language in
> which a mother first greets her new-born child, . . . the language which
> unites us with our fellow-men in happy fellowship or in serious business,
> the language, finally, in which our philanthropic and just king speaks to us,
> in which he proclaims his law to us.[12]

In 1845, Abraham Geiger, the great theoretician of the
Reform movement, felt constrained to confess that a German
prayer aroused in him deeper devotion than a Hebrew
prayer—and this in spite of the fact that, as he claimed, he
learned Hebrew before he learned German. But, for Geiger,
and in this he by no means stood alone among the Reformers
of the nineteenth century, the preference for German over
Hebrew as the language of prayer was much more than a

question as to which of the two languages can best express our deepest feelings and emotions. Rather was it a question about the very nature of Judaism itself. If Hebrew, so Geiger reasoned, is regarded as an essential element of Judaism, then Judaism would be forever stamped as a "national religion," seeing that a peculiar language is the mark of a separate national existence. Yet it was precisely the striving of Geiger and of his followers to usher in the new age when Jews would demonstrate, not least in their public worship services, that they had at last outgrown the national stage of their development.[13]

All of which would tend to prove that what the Reformers were really after was something quite different from the permission to pray in the vernacular, the kind of permission which the sources of Rabbinic law so obviously conceded them. Far from being an emergency measure to meet the situation of a contemporary failure in Hebrew education, the use of the vernacular in prayer was made a matter of ideology—of an ideology, moreover, which ran counter to what was then still the existential self-awareness of the vast majority of the Jewish people. Their Orthodox opponents must have instinctively felt this threat to Jewish peoplehood. That is why they reacted so violently—even though the logic of their argument no more related to this real and fundamental issue than the Reformers' invocation of Rabbinic permissions to pray in the vernacular truly expressed the Reformers' real ideological objective.

However, all that is in the distant past now—pre-Auschwitz and pre-State of Israel. Perhaps the time has finally come when the question of Hebrew and vernacular prayer can be faced on its own merits, without polemical and apologetic side glances. It is obvious, of course, as a matter of historical fact though not of halakhic theory, that Hebrew is the language of Jewish prayer. It is equally obvious that, as long as a sizable number of members does not understand Hebrew, non-Orthodox synagogues will continue to use the vernacular in varying degrees. The point, however, is that the congregations will have to understand that the use of the vernacular is a

makeshift arrangement, and that together with the use of the
vernacular, there must be intensive efforts in the field of
Hebrew education. Prayer in the vernacular can be tolerated
for purposes of greater intelligibility. It must be emphatically
rejected if it is to serve the purpose of not letting our worship
services look like being "too Orthodox," or even like being "too
Jewish." Prayer in the vernacular is neither virtuous nor
sinful. It is there for some very practical reasons. But it must
never become an ideology!

We cannot conclude this chapter on the languages of prayer
without drawing attention to the renaissance of Hebrew as
the spoken language of the State of Israel. There, Hebrew and
the vernacular are one and the same thing. There, needless to
say, Hebrew as the language of prayer can no longer serve the
purposes of mystification. There, the worshipper understands
the words on the printed page in front of him. Many of those
words, of course, lend themselves to poetic interpretation.
But, here and there, the Israeli worshipper may well
encounter a word or a phrase which does not so lend itself,
which, in fact, rings downright "untrue." In such instances we
may expect some Israelis—even among those who do not
describe themselves as Conservative or Reform—to clamor
for some changes in the wording of the traditional prayers.
Indeed, this has already happened—with reference to the
liturgical descriptions of Exile and of the pitiful state of
Jerusalem after the destruction. Some enlightened Orthodox
leaders in Israel have already met some of those demands.
(We may well be destined to witness some parallel developments in the liturgies of both Orthodox Judaism and the
Roman Catholic Church. The celebration of the Mass in the
vernacular, in the one case, and the recitation of prayers in a
holy language which has *become* the vernacular, in the other,
are bringing about the kind of situation in which traditionalist religions have to face the challenge of either meaning
what they are saying or of changing the wording of the
liturgy to make it correspond to what is "really" believed.)
But, in terms of the future of the Jewish prayer book, the

Hebrew-speaking environment of the State of Israel may even have more fundamental changes in store for us. At the end of his important volume on *Prayer in the Period of the Tannaim and the Amoraim,* Dr. Joseph Heinemann draws attention to the fact that the old Palestinian rite has throughout been marked by a greater freedom and variety than the Babylonian rite. Standardization, he claims, was the work of the *Babylonian,* not of the Palestinian, Sages. Involved here, according to Heinemann, was most certainly the tendency, characteristic of the Babylonian Sages as a whole, to systematize and to arrange all the details of private and of public life. But, continues Heinemann, of even greater import was the difficulty which the Jews of the diaspora experienced in the free creation of Hebrew prayer formulae. And they did not want to dispense with Hebrew—in spite of the permission granted by the *Mishnah* to recite the *Shema,* the Eighteen Benedictions, and the Grace after Meals "in any language." Insisting, in spite of that legal leniency, on prayer in Hebrew, the Babylonian Jews were gradually compelled to give up flexibility and innovations in their liturgy. The standardized rite was the price they had to pay for their love of Hebrew at a time when Hebrew was no longer a living language for them.[14]

When prayer in Hebrew was insisted on in non-Hebrew-speaking Babylonia, the Jew's love for Hebrew was clearly demonstrated. But he paid for it by giving up the greater variety and flexibility which used to be available on Palestinian soil. One may argue that the price was well worth paying. But one may also wonder whether rigorous standardization may not, after all, have been a distinctive diaspora phenomenon. And one may hope, if one is so inclined, that the combination of land, people and language, as we find it in the Land of Israel today, may again open up the wellsprings of Jewish liturgical creativity and spiritual regeneration. If that should come to pass, Hebrew will indeed have had the decisive say.

Chapter Six

CAN MODERN MAN PRAY?

The question is often asked: "Can modern man pray?" The simple truth is, of course, that some modern men can pray, while others cannot. That is, if by "modern man" we mean the man living in the second half of the twentieth century. We all know people who, for one reason or another, find it impossible to pray. And we all know those who, in spite of everything, continue to pray.

But, perhaps, when we say "modern," we do not so much refer to a specific date of the calendar, but rather to a frame of mind. Modern man, in this sense, is the sophisticated man, the man who is a college graduate, who has studied the physical sciences, philosophy and psychology—the man, in short, who has given up the so-called childish and naive "God concepts" of his presumably benighted ancestors. There are many such "modern men" who, if they tolerate a "God concept" at all, think in terms of a depersonalized Force which it is useless to approach in prayer, and which is oblivious to the spoken human word and the anguished human cry.

However, they are not the only "modern men." Other "modern men" continue to find it possible to ascribe personality to their God. The physicist Robert A. Millikan, who died in 1953, was such a "modern man." He was able to say to the other group of "modern men":

If you, in your conception, wish to identify God with nature, you must perforce attribute to Him everything found in nature, such as consciousness and personality, or better *super-consciousness* and *super-personality*. For you cannot possibly synthesize nature and leave out of it its most outstanding attributes—those which you know that you yourself possess.[1]

And sometimes one may well wonder whether we are not overdoing the "modern" aspect of the *problematik* of our "modernity." Some of the problems which trouble us are not

56

nearly as uniquely "modern" as occasionally we like to think.

Here, for example, is a formulation of the problem of prayer:

The reason which leads men to doubt the efficacy of prayer is the same as that which leads them to deny God's knowledge. Their argument is as follows: Either God has determined that a given person shall receive a given benefit, or He has not so determined. If He has determined, there is no need of prayer; and if He has not determined, how can prayer avail to change God's will that He should now determine to benefit the person, when He had not so determined before? For God does not change from a state of willing to a state of not willing, or vice versa. For this reason they say that right conduct is of no avail for receiving a good from God. And similarly they say that prayer does not avail to enable one to receive a benefit, or to be saved from an evil which has been decreed against him.[2]

Change a phrase here and there, and you have a very "modern" statement of the problem. With a sophisticated "God concept" up your sleeve, how can you possibly believe in the efficacy of prayer? Nevertheless, this particular formulation of the problem is not modern at all. It goes back to Joseph Albo, in the fifteenth century! Albo attempts to solve the problem by saying that the determined good or evil is conditional upon man's being righteous or wicked, and is liable to change to the extent to which man himself changes—with prayer and right conduct helping to prepare the person to change from the evil state in which he was.[3] This attempted solution may or may not satisfy us today. But there is no question that, in his *formulation* of the problem, Albo was no less "modern" than we are today.

Nor, with regard to prayer, do we find ourselves in a uniquely "modern" situation just because we are the witnesses of Auschwitz and all it stands for. The dimensions of the modern Holocaust are unprecedented. But, surely, the contemporaries of the destruction of Temple and State, in the year 70 c.e., might have been stunned by the same incomprehension with which we face Auschwitz. And the destruction of the First Temple seems to have given rise to similar reactions.

"Though I call and cry for help," we read in Lamentations

(3: 8), "He shuts out my prayer." And again (5: 19), "Why dost Thou forget us for ever, forsake us so long?" Still, for the authors of Lamentations, God did not die, or go into eclipse. If anything, their theology is even *more* radical. "The Lord has become like an *enemy*" (2: 5)! "He is to me like a bear lying in wait, like a lion in hiding. He led me off my ways, tore me to pieces, and made me desolate" (3: 10-11). And yet, when all is said and done, the whole thing is addressed *to* God! It culminates in the hope (5: 21) that God may restore us, so that we may be restored.

The Book of Lamentations, in fact, is a prayer. And it is a prayer precisely because, in full awareness of the utter misery and desolation of the moment, the poet is able to look beyond the present moment—to *dare* to look. For prayer is not the shutting of one's eyes to reality. It is the glimmer, the intimation, the daring which leads to the transcending of reality. Not all men, ancient or modern, have had the courage and the vision to do so. But those who established and carried on the classical tradition of Jewish prayer always did.

Auschwitz is an aspect of the perennial problem of theodicy; and the problem of theodicy creates difficulties not only with regard to prayer, but with regard to the belief in God itself. It is there when one single innocent human child is taken from us. It is there, multiplied by six million, in the Holocaust of our age. It surely can interfere with our ability to pray. But it need not necessarily do so. Indeed, it might even make our prayerful cry more heartrending, more rooted in the real human situation. But, in the light of millennia of Jewish martyrdom, this is hardly a particularly "modern" problem.

Finally, since the average Jew confronts the problem of prayer primarily within the context of public worship, a few words about the latter may be in order here. The complaint is often heard that public worship leaves modern Jews spiritually unsatisfied. But why is it that we expect the Jewish worship service to have an instant effect on the uninitiated participant (or, better, spectator), when we, quite rightly, presuppose just a little bit of musical education on the part of those who want to get something out of a Beethoven symphony or a Bach cantata? In addition to all the other things which the Jewish worship service is meant to be, the synagogue service, as a unit, also represents a poetic creation; and, like every other poetic creation, it requires some training in poetic appreciation. Once we acquire that appreciation, we shall be less likely to become victims of that literalist and pedestrian approach which has so often marked Reform Judaism's handling of the liturgical heritage of the past. Nor shall we require that the synagogue service always speak to us in the accents of the latest fashions in popular philosophy, psychology, and theology.

Moreover, once we understand the place of prayer within the structure of Jewish public worship, we shall also realize that, in the nature of the case, not all prayers could possibly appeal to all people at all times. In moments of ill health, for example, the prayer, "Heal us, O Lord, and we shall be healed," is more likely to make me linger over it than when I enjoy robust health. Perhaps all of our petitionary prayers should, in any case, be relegated to silent devotion. The time allocated for such silent devotion might well be increased. But the prayer book should have ample provisions for filling it.

This, however, is a problem of detail. More serious, on the other hand, are the claims occasionally voiced of late, that the prayer book go easy on the praise which it gives to God, because, so it is asserted, man also is entitled to a share of that praise. As we look around ourselves these days, we hardly find that man is undernourished in the sustenance feeding his own ego. He is so busy celebrating the secular city all over the place that he hardly needs the synagogue for an additional ego boost. It may well be the function of the synagogue, particularly during the Sabbath service, to remind man that it is *God* who gives him the strength to prosper and to achieve (Deuteronomy 8: 18). The religious, the Jewish approach, so far from lessening the praises of God because of man's achievements, is to perceive in the achievements of man a manifestation of the power of God. Any dichotomy introduced here is artificial, and not inherent in the liturgical material itself.

When Samuel Morse, in 1843, got his telegraph line working between Washington and Baltimore, it was a tremendous achievement, of which Morse could have been inordinately proud. No doubt he was. But the first message he sent was: "What hath God wrought!" Samuel Morse was closer to the true spirit of Jewish prayer than those who have compunctions about saying: "Through Thy power alone has Israel been redeemed from the hand of oppressors." Man's prayer of thanksgiving addressed to God has never been taken to imply that God does not work through human channels. But man's self-congratulatory prayer, addressed to man, is idolatry.

Still more serious is the attempt to revive an ancient heresy, which the Rabbis combatted when they prohibited the prayer: "May Thy Name be remembered for the good."[4] The heresy in question, both in ancient times and in modernity, is an unwillingness to credit God with the evil that befalls us. God is responsible for the good things in life. Evil and suffering are either the work of another deity, of recalcitrant matter, or a dysteleological surd. It is an attractive theory. It makes one's God concept so much more manageable; and it saves one from the embarrassment of having to admit that his God is liable to do things every once in a while which man cannot bring into line with his definition of the "God concept." By way of contrast, the classical Jewish approach, which regards God as "Fashioner of light and Creator of darkness, Maker of peace and Creator of evil" (Isaiah 45:7), though bristling with its own serious theological difficulties, at least witnesses to a God who is not unrelated to the tragic dimension of human existence.

By having taken note of some of the criticisms which have been voiced in connection with our public worship service, we have already encountered some of the problems which modern man faces with regard to prayer itself—public prayer or private prayer. While we have tried to show that a number of those problems are not nearly as "modern" as we occasionally like to think, we have also been able to discern the nature of our so-called "modern" difficulties. It seems to be taken for granted (a) that we are in need of a new "God concept," and (b) that prayer is only possible if it does not override the definitions of such a "God concept."

About the first assumption, that we are in need of a new "God concept," there is certainly, as yet, no unanimity. "God concepts" are, of course, a necessity—if only to make theological discourse possible. It is clear that, in order to be intelligible, "God concepts" will have to be formulated in different language at different times. But it is equally clear that, from the believer's point of view, "God concepts" do not exhaust the sphere of the Divine. God, to be God, must be bigger than man's concept of Him. The Rabbinic passage, which some of our rationalists are so fond of quoting, in which Rabbi Chaninah criticized an over-enthusiastic prayer leader, who had been heaping up the attributes of God, by ironically asking him, "Have you exhausted all the praises of your Lord?",[5] is a passage which is no less applicable to the architects of our "God concepts." "Have you," they might well be asked, "exhausted all the definitions of your Lord?"

The historian of religion and the philosopher of religion can and must operate with "God concepts." But the practising religionist needs a God who transcends human definitions—a God who is no more exhausted by the philosopher's definitions of Him than He is by the poet's lyrical heaping up of attributes. That is why the theologian fails so miserably the moment he loses sight of human limitations—and of his own sense of humor. The distinction between God and "God concept" is vital for the clarification of modern man's problem with prayer. It is harder to pray to a "God concept" than it is to pray to God.

Of course, the protagonist of a "God concept" will deny, and perhaps rightly so, that when he prays (and if he prays), he is addressing his concept rather than God Himself. Yet, to say the least, it is suggestive that it is from the circles of those who speak of "God concepts," rather than of God, that most of the proposals emanate to substitute meditation for prayer, and to speak of God in the third, rather than in the second person. Prayer appears to be something more primitive (not necessarily in the derogatory sense), more elemental and spontaneous. It is the cry wrung from the human heart, the aspiration of the human soul, the confidence of the human spirit, in the presence of the Holy One—even though the man who utters the prayer may not yet have defined the Holy One for himself, or theologized about Him. Israel in Egypt cries out to God—*before* Moses gives them more adequate information about His nature. And Moses himself prays *before* he obtains that information. In fact, he prays *for* that information (Exodus 33: 18).

The formation of "concepts" comes later. It is a more sophisticated and reflective stage in religious evolution. It would also appear to be connected with a different aspect of our own being than spontaneous prayer is. The immediacy is gone. "I—Thou" gives way to "I—It." In this connection, it is interesting to find that the prayers which originated in the House of Study *(bet hamidrash)*—as contrasted with those of Temple and synagogue origin, not to speak of the biblical Psalms—are prayers which refer to God in the third person: "May His great Name be praised," "Praised be He who says and does, promises and fulfils," "May the Holy One, praised be He, renew the new moon for us,"[6] etc.

It should, however, be understood that the Rabbis, who, in their *bet hamidrash,* created the prayer formula in the third person, also used prayer formulae which addressed God as "Thou." If the reflective mood induced by the House of Study was responsible for the circumlocutions, the Rabbis were, nevertheless, and continued to be believing Jews who never ceased to pray, "Praised art Thou, O Lord" *(barukh attah adonai).*

It is this combination of the reflective and the spontaneous, this harmonization of apparent irreconcilables, that has remained characteristic of Jewish prayer to this day. A Maimonides, despairing of the capacity of human language to do full justice to God—"for whatever we may say intending to magnify and exalt, on the one hand we find that it can have some application to Him, may He be exalted, and on the other we perceive in it some deficiency"—may regard silence and the "apprehensions of the intellect" as more appropriate.[7] But this does not prevent Maimonides either from accepting the prayers which, in his opinion, were composed by the Men of the Great Assembly,[8] or from devoting considerable space to the "Laws of Prayer" in his Code. And his son, Abraham, who must have enjoyed a thorough Maimonidean education, was known for his intensive liturgical concerns.[9]

Yet it is the co-existence of prayer and reflection, of "God concept" and religious belief in God, a co-existence taken for granted in the past, which "modern man" chooses to regard as a stumbling block to prayer. Unlike his ancestors, who affirmed both, "modern man" emphasizes an "either/or" dichotomy. Regarding himself as having graduated to the reflective stage, he tends to reject the notion that God Himself can be approached in prayer. It is in this context that the second "modern" assumption arises, i.e., that prayer is only possible if it does not override the definitions of our "God concept."

Here again, however, the requirement is not nearly as "modern" as, at first sight, it might seem. Already the Tannaim (the teachers in the days of the *Mishnah*) placed certain limitations upon prayer, limitations which could only have been due to the influence of a reflective "God concept" upon the nature of prayer. Says the *Tosephta:*

There are things which are a frivolous prayer (*tephillat tiphlah*). In what way? If a man brings in a hundred *khor* (of grain), and says, "May it be God's will that they be two hundred," or if he brings in a hundred barrels, and says, "May it be God's will that they be two hundred," then this is a vain prayer (*tephillat shav*). But he *may* pray, "Cause blessing to enter into them, and do not cause a curse to enter into them."[10]

And the *Mishnah* says:

If someone cries out over something that is past, then this is a vain prayer (*tephillat shav*). In what way? If his wife was pregnant, and he said, "May it be God's will that my wife give birth to a male child," then this is a vain prayer. If someone comes along the way, and he hears an outcry from the city, and he prays, "May it be God's will that those be not the members of my family," then this is a vain prayer.[11]

What is so particularly striking in those Tannaitic passages is the degree of sophistication which has led to the renunciation of that type of prayer. In theory, at least, the Rabbis prayed to the biblical God; and the God of the Bible is reported to have performed all kinds of miracles. He split the sea, He made the sun stand still for Joshua, He made iron float on water, and He made the sun dial go back ten steps for Hezekiah. The miracles asked for in the prohibited prayers of *Mishnah* and *Tosephta* are quite minor in comparison. Yet the Rabbis had become accustomed to living in a world in which the course of nature was, on the whole, no longer interrupted by supernatural interventions. "The world pursues its natural course." *(Olam keminhago noheg.)*[12] And this recognition led to the rejection of certain types of prayer as being "frivolous" and "vain." Prayer, in other words, even for the Rabbis, had its limitations derived from their "God concept."

Nor were those limitations imposed only by a more sophisticated view of nature. Historical experiences were taken into consideration as well. In one of the most daring passages of the Talmud, Jeremiah and Daniel are vindicated in spite of their alleged departures from the presumed traditional ritual, because, in all honesty, their own experiences made it impossible for them to ascribe certain attributes to God.

Moses had come and said: "The great God, the mighty, and the awe-inspiring" (Deuteronomy 10:17). Then Jeremiah came and said: "Aliens are destroying His Temple. Where, then, are His awe-inspiring deeds?" Therefore he omitted (in Jeremiah 32:17f.) the attribute of "awe-inspiring." Daniel came and said: "Aliens are enslaving His sons. Where are His mighty deeds?" Therefore he omitted (in Daniel 9:4ff.) the word "mighty." . . . But how could they abolish something established by Moses? Rabbi Eleazar said: "Since they knew that the Holy One, praised be He, insists on truth, they would not say untrue things about Him."[13]

It should be pointed out that this is not the Talmud's last word on the subject. The context of this passage deals with the reason why the Men of the Great Assembly were called "great." It was because they restored the "crown of divine attributes" to its former glory. Knowing as well as Jeremiah

and Daniel did about the catastrophic fate which had
overtaken their people, they—with a more profound insight
into the nature of God and of history—found it possible, after
all, to call God "mighty and awe-inspiring."

Still, the fact remains that, according to Rabbi Eleazar, the
quest for truth, understood as a divine mandate, is liable to
lead to changes in one's theology. And, in their turn, those
changes in theology justify changes in the nature of prayer.
Such a view, considering its time and place, should help us see
our own "modernity" in a little more perspective. Our age has
not been granted a monopoly on theological and liturgical
problems. Some of our most burning questions have been
faced before, long before. And the fact that, in spite of it (or,
perhaps, *because* of it), prayer has never ceased in Israel
might well make us pause before we jump to conclusions
about "modern man's" ability, or inability, to pray.

Yet, more even than with our "God concept, " the problem of
prayer (as distinct from the problem of meditation[14]) is
inextricably bound up with our view of *man*. If man is really a
self-sufficient creature, if he is in no need of support from a
Reality beyond himself, and if he is so self-sufficient that he
does not even look upon himself as a "creature," then, indeed,
man—ancient or modern—cannot pray. If, on the other hand,
man relies on spiritual strength and support coming from
outside of himself, if, that is to say, he knows himself to be a
creature, though he may also know himself to be needed by
God as a junior partner in the ongoing work of creation, then
modern man *can* pray.

If his be a prosaic frame of mind, he may encounter some
difficulties with the language and the imagery in which
earlier generations have couched their prayers. If, on the
other hand, he is gifted with poetic appreciation, then the
words of the prayer book will be an aid to him, and not a
stumbling block. But, in either case, "modern man," as
premodern man before him, must, from time to time, check
the contents of his prayers against the nature of his "God
concept," lest his prayers become "frivolous" and "vain." The
reach of prayer may, and should, outdistance the grasp of our

philosophical and theological definitions. God, to be God, must
be greater than our concepts of Him. But true prayer cannot
very well voice strivings and aspirations which run counter to
the very nature of God as we conceive of Him. This seems to
be the profound truth behind the Rabbinic requirement that
the creedal element of the Jewish worship service, i.e., the
recitation of the *Shema* and its Benedictions, *precede* the
prayer of petition.[15]

We have, in this chapter, been trying to provide some
perspective and background for the frequently asked question, "Can modern man pray?" We have seen that some of the
problems which trouble us are problems which have equally
troubled our predecessors. We have also noted that one's
ability to pray depends, in the final analysis, upon his ability
to see himself as a creature of God. There are those who have
this ability, and there are those who do not. But this "creature
feeling," this sense of one's absolute dependence upon God, is
not something which can be made the burden of rational
persuasion. That is why we have to end our answer as we have
begun it. Can modern man pray? Some can, and some cannot.

Part Two
MEANINGS AND DIRECTIONS:
AN ANTHOLOGY

Chapter Seven

ON PRAYER

ABRAHAM JOSHUA HESCHEL

Primarily my theme is not liturgy, public worship, public ritual, but rather private worship, prayer as an enterprise of the individual self, as a personal engagement, as an intimate, confidential act.

Public worship is an act of the highest importance. However, it tends in our days to become a spectacle, in which the congregation remains passive, inert spectators. But prayer is action; it requires complete mobilization of heart, mind, and soul. What is the worth of attending public worship when mind and soul are not involved? Renewal of liturgy involves renewal of prayer.

There is, in addition, a malady indigenous or congenital to liturgy. Liturgy as an act of prayer is an outcome and distillation of the inner life. Although its purpose is to exalt the life which engenders it, it harbors a tendency to follow a direction and rhythm of its own, independent of and divorced from the energies of life which brought prayer into being. At the beginning, liturgy is intimately related to the life which calls it into being. But as liturgy unfolds, it enters a state of stubborn disconnection, even into a state of opposition. Liturgy is bound to become rigid, to stand by itself, and to take on a measure of imperviousness. It tends to become timeless, transpersonal; liturgy for the sake of liturgy. Personal presence is replaced by mere attendance; instead of erecting a sanctuary of time in the realm of the soul, liturgy attracts masses of people to a sanctuary in the realm of space.

I do not wish to set up a dichotomy of prayer and liturgy. This would contradict the spirit of devotion. I merely wish to concentrate my thoughts on prayer as a personal affair, as an act of supreme importance. I plead for the primacy of prayer in our inner existence. The test of authentic theology is the degree to which it reflects and enhances the power of prayer, the way of worship.

In antiquity as well as in the Middle Ages, due to the scarcity of parchment, people would often write new texts on top of earlier written parchments. The term denoting such writings is *palimpsest*. Metaphorically, I suggest that authentic theology is a palimpsest: scholarly, disciplined thinking grafted upon prayer.

Prayer is either exceedingly urgent, exceedingly relevant, or inane and useless. Our first task is to learn to comprehend why prayer is an ontological necessity. God is hiding, and man is defying. Every moment God is creating and self-concealing. Prayer is disclosing or at least preventing irreversible concealing. God is ensconced in mystery, hidden in the depths. Prayer is pleading with God to come out of the depths. "Out of the depths have I called Thee, O Lord" (Psalms 130:1).

We have lost sensitivity to truth and purity of heart in the wasteland of opportunism. It is, however, a loss that rebounds to afflict us with anguish. Such anguish, when converted into prayer, into a prayer for truth, may evoke the dawn of God. Our agony over God's concealment is sharing in redeeming God's agony over man's concealment.

Prayer as an episode, as a cursory incident, will not establish a home in the land of oblivion. Prayer must pervade as a climate of living, and all our acts must be carried out as variations on the theme of prayer. A deed of charity, an act of kindness, a ritual moment—each is prayer in the form of a deed. Such prayer involves a minimum or even absence of outwardness, and an abundance of inwardness.

A Sanctuary for the Soul

Prayer is not a stratagem for occasional use, a refuge to resort to now and then. It is rather like an established residence for the innermost self. All things have a home, the bird has a nest, the fox has a hole, the bee has a hive. A soul without prayer is a soul without a home. Weary, sobbing, the soul, after roaming through a world festered with aimlessness, falsehoods and absurdities, seeks a moment in which to gather up its scattered life, in which to divest itself of enforced pretensions and camouflage, in which to simplify complexities, in which to call for help without being a coward. Such a home is prayer. Continuity, permanence, intimacy, authenticity, earnestness are its attributes. For the soul, home is where prayer is.

In his cottage, even the poorest man may bid defiance to misery and malice. That cottage may be frail, its roof may shake, the wind may blow through it, the storms may enter it, but there is where the soul expects to be understood. Just as the body, so is the soul in need of a home.

Everybody must build his own home; everybody must guard the independence and the privacy of his prayers. It is the source of security for the integrity of conscience, for whatever inkling we attain of eternity. At home I have a Father who judges and cares, who has regard for me, and when I fail and go astray, misses me. I will never give up my home.

What is a soul without prayer? A soul runaway or a soul evicted from its own home. To those who have abandoned their home: the road may be hard and dark and far, yet do not be afraid to steer back. If you prize grace and eternal meaning, you will discover them upon arrival.

How marvelous is my home. I enter as a suppliant and emerge as a witness; I enter as a stranger and emerge as next of kin. I may enter spiritually shapeless, inwardly disfigured, and emerge wholly changed. It is in moments of prayer that my image is forged, that my striving is fashioned. To understand the world I must love my home. It is difficult to perceive luminosity anywhere if there is no light in my own home. It is in the light of prayer's radiance that I find my way even in the dark. It is prayer that illumines my way. As my prayers, so is my understanding.

The Many Purposes of Prayer

Prayer serves many aims. It serves to save the inward life

from oblivion. It serves to alleviate anguish. It serves to partake of God's mysterious grace and guidance. Yet, ultimately, prayer must not be experienced as an act for the sake of something else. We pray in order to pray.

Prayer is a perspective from which to behold, from which to respond to the challenges we face. Man in prayer does not seek to impose his will upon God; he seeks to impose God's will and mercy upon himself. Prayer is necessary to make us aware of our failures, backsliding, transgressions, sins.

Prayer is more than paying attention to the holy. Prayer comes about as an event. It consists of two inner acts: an act of turning and an act of direction. I leave the world behind as well as all interests of the self. Divested of all concerns, I am overwhelmed by only one desire: to place my heart upon the altar of God.

God is beyond the reach of finite notions, diametrically opposed to our power of comprehension. In theory He seems to be neither here nor now. He is so far away, an outcast, a refugee in His own world. It is as if all doors were closed to Him. To pray is to open a door, where both God and soul may enter. Prayer is arrival, for Him and for us. To pray is to overcome distance, to shatter screens, to render obliquities straight, to heal the break between God and the world. A dreadful oblivion prevails in the world. The world has forgotten what it means to be human. The gap is widening, the abyss is within the self.

Though often I do not know how to pray, I can still say: Redeem me from the agony of not knowing what to strive for, from the agony of not knowing how my inner life is falling apart.

A candle of the Lord is the soul of man, but the soul can become a holocaust, a fury, a rage. The only cure is to discover that over and above the anonymous stillness in the world there is a Name and a waiting.

Many young people suffer from a fear of the self. They do not feel at home in their own selves. The inner life is a place of dereliction, a no man's land, inconsolate, weird. The self has become a place from which to flee. The use of narcotic drugs is a search for a home.

Human distress, wretchedness, agony, is a signal of a universal distress. It is a sign of human misery; it also proclaims a divine predicament. God's mercy is too great to permit the innocent to suffer. But there are forces that interfere with God's mercy, with God's power. This is a dreadful mystery as well as a challenge: God is held in captivity.

I pray because God, the *Shekhinah,* is an outcast. I pray because God is in exile, because we all conspire to blur all signs of His presence in the present or in the past. I pray because I refuse to despair, because extreme denials and defiance are refuted in the confrontation of my own presumption and the mystery all around me. *I pray because I am unable to pray.*

And suddenly I am forced to do what I seem unable to do. Even callousness to the mystery is not immortal. There are moments when the clamor of all sirens dies, presumption is depleted, and even the bricks in the walls are waiting for a song. The door is closed, the key is lost. Yet the new sadness of my soul is about to open the door.

Some souls are born with a scar, others are endowed with anesthesia. Satisfaction with the world is base and the ultimate callousness. The remedy for absurdity is still to be revealed. The irreconcilable opposites which agonize human existence are the outcry, the prayer. Every one of us is a cantor; everyone of us is called to intone a song, to put into prayer the anguish of all.

God is in captivity in this world, in the oblivion of our lives. God is in search of man, in search of a home in the soul and deeds of man. God is not at home in our world. Our task is to hallow time, to enable Him to enter our moments, to be at home in our time, in what we do with time.

Ultimately, prayer in Judaism is an act in the messianic drama. We utter the words of the *Kaddish: Magnified and sanctified be His great name in the world which He has created according to His will.* Our hope is to enact, to make real the magnification and sanctification of this name here and now.

A great mystery has become a reality in our own days, as God's response to a people's prayer. After nearly two thousand years the city of David, the city of Jerusalem, is now restored to the people of Israel. This marvelous event proclaims a call for the renewal of worship, for the revival of prayer. We did not enter the city of Jerusalem on our own in 1967. Streams of endless craving, endless praying, clinging, dreaming, day and night, midnights, years, decades, centuries, millenia, streams of tears, pledging, waiting—from all over the world, from all corners of the earth, carried us of this generation to the Wall, to the city of Jerusalem.

Prayer is Living

Prayer must not be dissonant with the rest of living. The mercifulness, gentleness, which pervades us in moments of prayer is but a ruse or a bluff, if it is inconsistent with the way we live at other moments. The divorce of liturgy and living, of prayer and practice, is more than a scandal; it is a disaster. A word uttered in prayer is a promise, an earnest, a commitment. If the promise is not kept, we are guilty of violating a promise. A liturgical revival cannot come about in isolation. Worship is the quintessence of living. Perversion or suppression of the sensibilities that constitute being human will convert worship into a farce. What is handicapping prayer is not the antiquity of the Psalms but our own crudity and spiritual immaturity.

The hour calls for a revision of fundamental religious concerns. The wall of separation between the sacred and the secular has become a wall of separation between the conscience and God. In the Pentateuch, the relation of man to things of space, to money, to property is a fundamental religious problem. In the affluent society sins committed with money may be as grievous as sins committed with our tongue. We will give account for what we have done, for what we have failed to do.

Religion as an establishment must remain separated from the government. Yet prayer as a voice of mercy, as a cry for justice, as a plea for gentleness, must not be kept apart. Let the spirit of prayer dominate the world. Let the spirit of prayer interfere in the affairs of man. Prayer is private, a service of the heart; but let concern and compassion, born out of prayer, dominate public life.

Prayer is a confrontation with Him who demands justice and compassion, with Him who despises flattery and abhors iniquity. Prayer calls for self-reflection, for contrition and repentance, examining and readjusting deeds and motivations, for recanting the ugly compulsions we follow, the tyranny of acquisitiveness, hatred, envy, resentment. We face not only things—continents, oceans, planets. We also face a claim, an expectation.

God reaches us as a claim. Religious responsibility is responsiveness to the claim. He brought us into being; He brought us out of slavery. And He demands.

Heaven and earth were known to all men. Israel was given a third reality, the reality of the claim of the word of God. The task of the Jew is a life in which the word becomes deed. A sacred deed is where heaven and earth meet.

We have no triumphs to report except the slow, painstaking effort to redeem single moments in the lives of single men, in the lives of small communities. We do not come on the clouds of heaven but grope through the mists of history.

There is a pressing urgency to the work of justice and compassion. As long as there is a shred of hatred in a human heart, as long as there is a vacuum without compassion anywhere in the world, there is an emergency.

Why do people rage? People rage and hurt and do not know how to regret, how to repent. The problem is not that people have doubts, but rather people may not even care to doubt. The charity we may do is terribly diminutive compared with what is required. You and I have prayed, have craved to be able to make gentleness a certainty, and have so often failed. But there are in the world so many eyes streaming with tears, hearts dumb with fears, that to be discouraged would be treason.

Pray to be Shocked

The predicament of prayer is twofold: Not only do we not know how to pray; we do not know what to pray for.

We have lost the ability to be shocked.

The malignity of our situation is increasing rapidly, the magnitude of evil is spreading furiously, surpassing our ability to be shocked. The human soul is too limited to experience dismay in proportion to what has happened in Auschwitz, in Hiroshima.

We do not know what to pray for. Should we not pray for the ability to be shocked at atrocities committed by man, for the capacity to be dismayed at our inability to be dismayed?

Prayer should be an act of catharsis, of purgation of emotions, as well as a process of self-clarification, of examining priorities, of elucidating responsibility. Prayer not verified by conduct is an act of desecration and blasphemy. Do not take a word of prayer in vain. Our deeds must not be a refutation of our prayers.

It is with shame and anguish that I recall that it was possible for a Roman Catholic church adjoining the extermination camp in Auschwitz to offer communion to the officers of the camp, to people who day after day drove thousands of people to be killed in the gas-chambers.

Let there be an end to the separation of church and God, of sacrament and callousness, of religion and justice, of prayer and compassion.

A home is more than an exclusive habitat, mine and never yours. A residence devoid of hospitality is a den or a hole, not a home. Prayer must never be a citadel for selfish concerns, but rather a place for deepening concern over other people's plight. Prayer is a privilege. Unless we learn how to be worthy, we forfeit the right and ability to pray.

Prayer is meaningless unless it is subversive, unless it seeks to overthrow and to ruin the pyramids of callousness, hatred, opportunism, falsehoods. The liturgical movement must become a revolutionary movement, seeking to over-

throw the forces that continue to destroy the promise, the
hope, the vision.

The world is aflame with evil and atrocity; the scandal of
perpetual desecration of the world cries to high heaven. And
we, coming face to face with it, are either involved as callous
participants or, at best, remain indifferent onlookers. The
relentless pursuit of our interests makes us oblivious of
reality itself. Nothing we experience has value in itself;
nothing counts unless it can be turned to our advantage, into
a means for serving our self-interests.

We pray because the disproportion of human misery and
human compassion is so enormous. We pray because our
grasp of the depth of suffering is comparable to the scope of
perception of a butterfly flying over the Grand Canyon. We
pray because of the experience of the dreadful incompatibility
of how we live and what we sense.

Dark is the world to me, for all its cities and stars. If not for
my faith that God in His silence still listens to a cry, who
could stand such agony?

Prayer will not come about by default. It requires
education, training, reflection, contemplation. It is not
enough to join others; it is necessary to build a sanctuary
within, brick by brick, instants of meditation, moments of
devotion. This is particularly true in an age when overwhelming forces seem to conspire at destroying our ability to pray.

Prayer is Praise

The beginning of prayer is praise. The power of worship is
song. First we sing, then we understand. First we praise, then
we believe. Praise and song open eyes to the grandeur of
reality that transcends the self. Song restores the soul; praise
repairs spiritual deficiency.

To praise is to make Him present to our minds, to our
hearts, to vivify the understanding that beyond all questions,
protests, and pain at God's dreadful silence, is His mercy and
humility. We are stunned when we try to think of His essence;
we are exalted when intuiting His presence.

While it is true that being human is verified in relations between man and man, depth and authenticity of existence are disclosed in moments of worship.

Worship is more than paying homage. To worship is to join the cosmos in praising God. The whole cosmos, every living being sings, the Psalmists insist. Neither joy now sorrow but song is the ground-plan of being. It is the quintessence of life. To praise is to call forth the promise and presence of the divine. We live for the sake of a song. We praise for the privilege of being. Worship is the climax of living. There is no knowledge without love, no truth without praise. At the beginning was the song, and praise is man's response to the never-ending beginning.

The alternative to praise is disenchantment, dismay.

Society today is no longer in revolt against particular laws which it finds alien, unjust, and imposed, but against law as such, against the principle of law. And yet, we must not regard this revolt as entirely negative. The energy that rejects many obsolete laws is an entirely positive impulse for renewal of life and law.

"Choose life!" is the great legacy of the Hebrew Bible, and the cult of life is affirmed in contemporary theology. However, life is not a thing, static and final. Life means living, and in living you have to choose a road, direction, goals. Pragmatists who believe that life itself can provide us with the criteria for truth overlook the fact that forces of suicide and destruction are also inherent in life.

The essence of living as a human being is being challenged, being tempted, being called. We pray for wisdom, for laws of knowing how to respond to our being challenged. Living is not enough by itself. Just to be is a blessing. Just to live is holy. And yet, being alive is no answer to the problems of living. To be or not to be is *not* the question. The vital question is: how to be and how not to be?

The tendency to forget this vital question is the tragic disease of contemporary man, a disease that may prove fatal, that may end in disaster. To pray is to recollect *passionately* the perpetual urgency of this vital question.

The Uphill Struggle

One of the results of the rapid depersonalization of our age is a crisis of speech, profanation of language. We have trifled with the name of God, we have taken the name and the word of the Holy in vain. Language has been reduced to labels, talk has become double-talk. We are in the process of losing faith in the reality of words.

Yet prayer can only happen when words reverberate with power and inner life, when uttered as an earnest, as a promise. On the other hand, there is a high degree of obsolescence in the traditional language of the theology of prayer. Renewal of prayer calls for renewal of language, of cleansing the words, of revival of meanings.

The strength of faith is in silence, and in words that hibernate and wait. Uttered faith must come out as surplus of silence, as the fruit of lived faith, of enduring intimacy.

Theological education must deepen privacy, strive for daily renewal of innerness, cultivate ingredients of religious existence, *reverence* and *responsibility*.

We live in an age of self-dissipation, of depersonalization. Should we adjust our vision of existence to our paucity, make a virtue of obtuseness, glorify evasion?

My own sense of the reality of food depends upon my being hungry, upon my own craving for food. Had I grown up on intravenous food injections, apples and beans would be as relevant to me as pebbles and garbage.

Do we know how to thirst for God? Do we know what it means to starve?

> *O God, thou art my God, I seek Thee,*
> *my soul thirsts for Thee;*
> *my flesh faints for Thee,*
> *as in a dry and weary land where no water is.*
> *So I have looked upon Thee in the sanctuary,*
> *beholding Thy power and glory.*

Because Thy steadfast love is better than life,
my lips will praise Thee.
So I will bless Thee as long as I live;
I will lift up my hands and call on Thy name.

Psalms 63: 2-4

As a hart longs for flowing streams,
so longs my soul for Thee, O God.
My soul thirsts for God,
for the living God.
When shall I come and behold the face of God?
My tears have been my food day and night,
while men say to me continually,
"Where is your God?"

Psalms 42: 2-4

Religion is critique of all satisfaction. Its end is joy, but its beginning is discontent, detesting boasts, smashing idols. It began in Ur Kasdim, in the seat of a magnificent civilization. Yet Abraham said, "No," breaking the idols, breaking away. And so everyone of us must begin saying "No" to all visible, definable entities pretending to be triumphant, ultimate. The ultimate is a challenge, not an assertion. Dogmas are allusions, not descriptions.

Standing before Mt. Sinai, Israel was told: "Take heed that you do not go up to the mountain and touch the border of it." Take heed that you do not go up to the mountain and only touch the border. Go to the peak! Once you start going, proceed to the very end. Don't stop in the middle of the road.

This is the predicament of man. All souls descend a ladder from Heaven to this world. Then the ladders are taken away. Once they are in this world, they are called upon from Heaven to rise, to come back. It is a call that goes out again and again. Each soul seeks the ladder in order to ascend above; but the ladder cannot be found. Most people make no effort to ascend, claiming, how can one rise to heaven without a ladder? However, there are souls which resolve to leap upwards, without a ladder. So they jump and fall down. They jump and fall down, until they stop.

Wise people think that since no ladder exists, there must be another way. We must face the challenge and act. Be what it may, one must leap until God, in His mercy, makes exultation come about.

What do we claim? That religious commitment is not just an ingredient of the social order, an adjunct or reinforcement of existence, but rather the heart and core of being human; its exaltation, its verification being manifest in the social order, in daily deeds.

We begin with a sense of wonder and arrive at radical amazement. The first response is reverence and awe, openness to the mystery that surrounds us. We are led to be overwhelmed by the awareness of eternity in daily living.

Religious existence is living in solidarity with God. Yet to maintain such solidarity involves knowing how to rise, how to cross an abyss. Vested interests are more numerous than locusts, and of solidarity of character there is only a smattering. Too much devotion is really too little. It is grave self-deception to assume that our destiny is just to be human. In order to be human, one must be more than human. A person must never stand still. He must always rise, he must always climb. Be stronger than you are.

Well-trodden ways lead into swamps. There are no easy ways, there are no simple solutions. What comes easy is not worth a straw. It is a tragic error to assume that the world is flat, that our direction is horizontal. The way is always vertical. It is either up or down; we either climb or fall. Religious existence means struggle uphill.

Shattering the Silence

Life is a drama, and religion has become routine. The soul calls for exaltation, and religion offers repetition. Honesty, veracity does not come about by itself. Freshness, depth has to be acquired. One must work on it constantly.

To be moderate in the face of God would be a profanation. The goal is not an accommodation but a transformation. A mediocre response to immensity, to eternity, is offensive.

The tragedy of our time is that we have moved out of the dimension of the holy, that we have abandoned the intimacy in which relationship to God can be patiently, honestly, persistently nourished. Intimate inner life is forsaken. Yet the soul can never remain a vacuum. It is either a vessel for grace or it is occupied by demons.

At first men sought mutual understanding by taking counsel with one another, but now we understand one another less and less. There is a gap between the generations. It will soon widen to be an abyss. The only bridge is to pray together, to consult God before seeking counsel with one another. Prayer brings down the walls which we have erected between man and man, between man and God.

For centuries Jerusalem lay in ruins; of the ancient glory of King David and Solomon only a Wall remained, a stone Wall left standing after the Temple was destroyed by the Romans. For centuries Jews would go on a pilgrimage to Jerusalem in order to pour out their hearts at the Wailing Wall.

A wall stands between man and God, and at the wall we must pray, searching for a cleft, for a crevice, through which our words can enter and reach God behind the wall. In prayer we must often knock our heads against the stone wall. But God's silence does not go on forever. While man is busy setting up screens, thickening the wall, prayer may also succeed in penetrating the wall.

The tragedy is that many of us do not even know how to find the way leading to the wall. We of this generation are afflicted with a severe case of dulling or loss of vision. Is it the result of our own intoxication, or is it the result of God's deliberate concealment of visible lights?

The spiritual memory of many people is empty, words are diluted, incentives are drained, inspiration is exhausted. Is God to be blamed for all this? Is it not man who has driven Him out of our hearts and minds? Has not our system of religious education been an abysmal failure?

The spiritual blackout is increasing daily. Opportunism prevails, callousness expands, the sense of the holy is melting away. We no longer know how to resist the vulgar, how to say no in the name of a higher yes. Our roots are in a state of decay. We have lost the sense of the holy.

This is an age of spiritual blackout, a blackout of God. We have entered not only the dark night of the soul, but also the dark night of society. We must seek out ways of preserving the strong and deep truth of a living God theology in the midst of the blackout.

For the darkness is neither final nor complete. Our power is first in waiting for the end of darkness, for the defeat of evil; and our power is also in coming upon single sparks and occasional rays, upon moments full of God's grace and radiance.

We are called to bring together the sparks to preserve single moments of radiance and keep them alive in our lives, to defy absurdity and despair, and to wait for God to say again: Let there be light.

And there will be light.

Chapter Eight

SPEECH AND SILENCE BEFORE GOD[1]

STEVEN S. SCHWARZSCHILD

I.

The Jewish worship-service proper begins when the leader in prayer, addressing the congregation, chants the invitation: "Praise ye the Lord who is ultimately praised!"[2] The sentence is chanted very slowly so that during its recitation every worshipper will have the opportunity to bow and to whisper softly a short prayer (which never found a place in all prayer books in the first place, and which has unfortunately disappeared from many others since) that ends with the sentence taken from Nehemiah 9:5: "His Name is elevated above all praises and blessings."[3] The public invitation and the private prayers end at the same time, and then all join in responding to the invitation: "Praised is the Lord who is ultimately praised forever and ever." Thereupon the service as such commences.

This is an extraordinary and paradoxical declaration: on the one hand, the worshipper proclaims that God is so great that, as it were, no praise can do justice to Him. The logical conclusion to be drawn from such a recognition would be to refrain from trying to praise Him. But, on the other hand, the worshipper immediately proceeds to do that which he has just stated to be impossible: he praises Him.

The same liturgical paradox occurs in one of the most famous of all Jewish prayers, the *Kaddish*. This is one extended and rather wordy praise of God—a "doxology." Into the middle of it there is inserted the statement: "Let the Name of the Holy One, praised by He, be praised and acclaimed and exalted and elevated and uplifted and glorified

84

and upraised and adored—though It is above (on the High Holy Days: and yet above) all praise and song and acclamation and consolation that are said on earth,—to which ye say: Amen."

To believe in God is usually associated in our minds with praying to Him. Actually, silence before Him is at least as appropriate a stance. There are two possible reasons for such a silence, one which results from the nature of man, the other which results from the nature of God.

In the first sense, man's most profound emotions, his deepest needs and highest aspirations are embedded so tightly in the mine of his soul that the pick-axe of words cannot quite reach them. If God is to take cognizance of them at all, man can do no more than simply stand before Him and confidently hope that, out of His power and goodness, He will concern Himself with them. Psalms 4: 5: "Commune in your hearts on your beds and be still!" Psalms 139: 4: "There is no word on my tongue, but You, O God, know it all." It is in this kind of silence that lovers sit and perhaps hold hands, exchanging no vocal expressions but drinking in one another's presence. It is also this kind of silence that prevails between members of a family who have just lost a common and beloved relative: they look at one another and, weeping, perhaps bemoan their loss, but words could neither help them nor properly express their sentiments.

Such silence is itself due to two causes. In the first place, what goes on in the heart is so powerful, so inchoate, and so deeply chiseled into the flesh that even if it could be lifted out of its setting, it would break the delicate vessels of any words into which it might be put. In the second place, speech requires distance between the speaker and him who is addressed. None would think of using the telephone to communicate with a person who is sitting in the same room. Even so, we do not talk with anyone who is in our hearts. He knows what we feel while we feel it.[4]

Two examples of liturgical inarticulateness come to mind. For twenty-five hours the Jew has prayed out his heart and mind on the Day of Atonement. When evening comes and the long fast draws to a close, tens of thousands of words must have been spoken and sung. And yet somehow we still feel that we have not penetrated to the heart of the matter; there are further unspoken feelings buried in us and interior courts in God's palace which we have not yet entered. Therefore, we muster the remaining physical and spiritual forces left under our command and make one last, desparate effort to descend into the human depths and to climb to the divine heights. But words have earlier proved futile. We cry out the *Shema,*—we repeat "Praised is the Name of the glory of His Kingdom" three times—and we stammer, each time at a higher and, as it were, more urgent pitch, seven times over the three Hebrew words: "The Lord, He is God." No longer is it the meaning of the words but rather their rhythm, the scream of the soul that squeezes through them, the hammering of their insistent repetition, in which we place our hope.[5] And, as if even this last resort had failed, finally we abandon the human voice and verbal expression altogether. We reach for the *shofar* and blow one long, piercing shriek: *teki'ah gedolah*—"This, surely, must rend the heavens."

Lest it be thought that the fallible frustrations of human prayer are the only causes that lead to worshipping silence, we must also remember the hasidic *niggunim,* the wordless chants into which unbounded joy before God can be, and often is poured. This, too, can exceed verbal capacity. Indeed, even the chant may be too restricted by the demands of rhythm, harmony, and continuity, and so cannot give vent to the fulness of religious intoxication—and then the entire human body begins to pray silently, moving and waving: "Let all my bones say: 'Who is like unto Thee!'"

"That which can be seen is lifted above and beyond human language. Light does not speak; it shines. It does not shut itself away, for it does not, after all, shine for itself, but rather toward the exterior. And its effulgence does not spend the light, as language spends itself in being spoken; the light does not give itself away as it gives of itself, nor does it deprive itself of itself as language does when it speaks; but, rather, it is visible while remaining itself. Actually it does not give off brightness; it merely shows brightness. It shines not like a well but like a countenance, as an eye shines that becomes eloquent without having to open the lips. Here is a silence which does not lack words like the dumbness of pre-humanity, but which simply does not need words any more. It is the silence of perfect understanding. Here a glance says everything. That the world is unredeemed is taught most clearly by the multiplicity of languages. Between men who speak a common language a glance suffices to bring about understanding; they do not need language precisely because they have a common language. But between different languages only the halting word mediates, and the gesture ceases to represent immediate comprehension as was the case with the silent glance of the eye; instead, it degenerates into the stammering of the language of gestures, this miserable emergency measure of communication. Thus it is that the highest level of the liturgy is not the common word but the common gesture. The liturgy redeems the gesture from the chains of being the awkward servant of language, and makes it into something more than language. Only the liturgical gesture anticipates the 'purified lip' which is promised for 'that day' to the peoples historically separated by their languages. In it the stark dumbness of the unbelieving limbs becomes eloquent, and the overflowing wordiness of the believing heart turns quiet. Unbelief and belief unite their prayer."[6]

II.

R. Aharon Rote, known as R. Arele, was an almost unknown hasidic mystic who died about twenty years ago.[7] The small group of his followers who today live in the Orthodox quarter of Me-ah She'arim in Jerusalem, largely identified with the "fanatical" group of *Natoré Kartha,* live in the kind of abysmal poverty, solely devoted to their religious exercises and studies, which also the founder of the group experienced throughout his life. (It must be added that neither in their personal behavior nor in their writings do they manifest any of the intolerant and aggressive fanaticism which is commonly attributed to them; rather the opposite is the case: they are most hospitable physically as well as religiously.) In his book, *Shomer Emunim*, R. Arele discusses silence before God several times.

"The Besht, may his merit protect us, said: 'If a man is in trouble or in danger, Heaven forfend, then the superlative thing to do is not to pray any kind of prayer. Let him only fortify his strong confidence in God, showing that he does not even possess the power any more to pray. Thus he will be like a little baby that does not even have the understanding to ask for anything; it is rather as Psalm 131 puts it: *My soul is like the weaned child upon its mother.* Thus also will he awaken the source of the faithfulness of the Godhead.'"

R. Arele refers to two talmudic passages which seem to him to support this advice to abstain from prayer under conditions of distress. *Berakhoth* 10a states: "R. Yochanan and R. Eleazar both said: 'Even when a sharp sword is placed upon a man's neck, let him not deprive himself of the quality of mercy, as it is written in Job 13: "Even if He slay me, yet will I trust in Him."'" R. Arele understandably asks: why is it regarded as even possible that a man, when his life is at stake, should abstain from asking for mercy? The implication clearly is, he reasons, that one might not ask explicitly for mercy, but, instead, silently and simply strengthen one's confidence that God will help.[8] He also directs attention to *Berakhoth* 5a. Here R. Yochanan makes the statement that "loving afflictions" are also those which do not involve the impossibility of study, thus implying, contrary to his polemical opponent, that sufferings which do involve the impossibility of prayer are, in turn, "afflictions of love."[9]

R. Arele returns to the same theme several times: inability to pray and abstinence from prayer are marks of the truly pious person. "It was furthermore written in the name of the Besht, may his memory be for blessing, that if a man gets into some kind of trouble, Heaven forfend and may it not happen, then it is the best thing not to pray at all at that time about his troubles. Let him merely very much strengthen his heart in God with trust in his Lord, for then 'Israel will be saved by God.'" Or again, reference is made to *Sepher Toledoth Adam,* portion *Vayiggash,* where the Besht is cited: "At a time when, Heaven forfend, judgment hangs over a man, let him not pray for the nullification of the verdict; let him only engage in thought, so that he may, perchance, not be further accused." Yet again, *Midrash Pinchas,* par. 157, is quoted: "I have heard it said in his name that if some trouble, Heaven forfend, befalls a man, may God help us, and he is really distressed, then there is no cure other than to trust in the grace of the Highest Who will not fail. Let him not do anything; let him look for no medicine;[10] let him only trust. Let him even not pray to the Holy One, praised be He, nor go to the ritual bath, or anything like this. Let him only trust."[11] Or, finally, once more: "And I, the lowly one who is writing this, in turn have experienced this myself any number of times, and I have found this advice of the Besht, may his merit protect us, wondrous."[12]

Here, clearly, was a man who knew, who must have experienced, what real anguish is. He says: if you can still pray, you are not really in trouble yet, for you still have the strength to pray. You are in real trouble when you cannot pray any more. But this lowest point in human existence, precisely because it is the lowest, is also closest to salvation. You cannot help yourself any more; now God must, and will, help. The birth-pangs of redemption must precede redemption. R. Arele had learned that human anguish and despair—not the mindless exhilaration which is usually attributed to Hasidism—are the existential situation in which God may be encountered. No doubt, Jewish experience of the millennia and the Jewish history of his own time, the time of Nazism over Europe, went into this recognition. The reality of death and of earthly misery stared him in the face at all times.

It is well-known that the philosophical and literary existentialists at the end of the Second World War explored and analyzed the experience of anguish, despair, and dread. Kierkegaard had written of the "despair which is the sickness

unto death" and of "the concept of dread." Heidegger had
spoken of the dread which "is involved in being-in-the-world.
It corresponds to the fact that we are ill-at-ease in the world,
not at home there."[13] Sartre describes the "dreadful freedom"
which "cannot but evoke anguish." "I emerge alone and in
anguish in face of the unique and primary object that
constitutes my being."[14] Or, he declares: ". . . forlornness
and anguish go together."[15] R. Arele is unlikely to have
known of Kierkegaard, and he certainly never sat in the
university halls of Heidelberg or the *café* houses of Paris. Yet,
what more overpowering definition of despair is conceivable
than that it is the state in which man cannot any more pray?

III.

The doctrine of "silence before God" may also help to
explain one of the most puzzling statements in all of Jewish
literature. Among Maimonides' most famous theories is the
thesis that God ordained the cult of sacrificial animals in the
Bible only as a concession to human weakness. For all sorts of
reasons Maimonides obviously was not enamored of bloody
sacrifices: they involve disregard of the humanitarian
prohibition to inflict "pain on living beings"; his Hellenistic
tendency toward intellectual and spiritualizing emphasis
would perforce be somewhat antagonized by them; and they
resemble pagan practices too much. Yet here they were,
divinely laid down in the Bible, and he had to come to terms
with them. He does so by assigning to them a historico-psychological reason (as he did with many other biblical
commandments): the Jews, like all other peoples of the
ancient world, were so accustomed to the idea that divine
worship could only be conducted by bringing animal sacrifices
that it would have been too much of a shock to them to have to
discard them suddenly and altogether. Instead, God reduced
their types and number, and restricted them to only one place.
(Even on its own terms, there is an inherent self-contradiction
in this doctrine: presumably it declares that God's purpose
was to abolish the sacrificial cult increasingly, gradually to

habituate Israel to the idea of doing without it. In this sense, the destruction of the Temple and, with it, the *de facto* elimination of sacrifices was the next big step, after the intermediary stage in which the Prophets re-emphasized the relationship between rite and righteousness, in the divine education of the Jewish people. In that case, certainly by the arrival of the Messiah, it should be made completely supererogatory. But the opposite is true: the Messiah will restore it. Indeed, Maimonides' own *Mishneh Torah* is sometimes suspected of having intended messianic purposes by including the sacrificial laws which other codes—of a more practical nature—had omitted.)

In connection with this theory, now, that the sacrifices were instituted by the Bible as a concession to human habituation and inertia, Maimonides makes a famous and extraordinary statement *(Guide to the Perplexed,* III, chapter 32): If God had ordained the elimination of the sacrifices, "this would then be as if a prophet were to come, in this our time, who called to the service of God by saying: 'The Lord has commanded you that you do not pray to Him, and that you do not fast, and that you do not implore His help in time of trouble, but rather that your service (of Him) consist (only) of thought without action.'"

What Maimonides meant to say is clear enough: it might have been theoretically preferable to spiritualize worship to the point of eliminating sacrifices, but practically this would have been too much to expect of human beings of flesh and blood, used to the old ways of the world; to have acted otherwise would be comparable to a prophetic demand in our time (when sacrifices are no longer brought because there is no Temple) that worship be spiritualized even further and dispense with such material aspects as verbalization, fasting, and self-interest, as do, for example, some of the Quakers. This, again, mortal human beings, still steeped in the materiality which characterizes our age, cannot reasonably be expected to bear. The equally clear implication of this statement seems, however, never to have been spelled out by the commentators. Maimonides, in this passage, regards sacrifices as a concession to human weakness which, ideally, should be overcome. By the same token, if the analogy is to have any validity, he must also have meant that spoken prayers, not to speak of fasts, are no more than a concession to human weakness, and should also ideally be discarded! From our modern vantage point, we may sympathize with his obvious distaste for animal sacrifices and, therefore, be prepared to accept his argument with respect to them—however respectful and mystified we may feel in the presence of the relevant biblical legislation. But how is one to explain that the twelfth-century philosopher and legalist went so far as not to disguise too darkly his thought that the institution of prayer, the very pillar on which religious Judaism in Bible, Talmud, and throughout the ages, rests—that this institution, too, is no more than a concession to human weakness which we should strive eventually to leave behind? Does he not himself authoritatively declare:

It is a positive commandment to pray every day, as it is said: "And ye shall serve the Lord your God!" and orally they were taught by God that this "service" refers to prayer, as it is said: "And to serve Him with all your heart." The Sages said: "What is the service of the heart? It is prayer."[16]

There is an answer to this problem in Maimonidean exegesis in terms of his philosophical system. It is part of his "negative theology." God is so great and unique that any words which people might use in relationship to God, and which would always perforce have to reflect their human sensuous experiences, would be offensive.[17] Therefore, even as the absence of sacrifices would be ideally preferable, so also silence before God would theoretically be more fitting than words. In the relevant context, Maimonides puts it this way:

The best thing said on this subject was said by the Psalms: "To Thee silence is praise." Psalms 65: 2.) The interpretation is that silence with reference to Thee is laudation, for everything that we might say, though we intend with it magnification and laudation, there is always connected with it something that besmirches the rank of the Highest, and we can detect in it a degree of inadequacy.[18]

However, in the last analysis, this philosophical explana-

tion of Maimonides' extraordinary statement is not completely satisfactory: (1) One is always left a bit stranded by
Maimonides' historico-psychological "reasons for the commandments." When these reasons have vanished, as surely
they have in the case of the sacrifices, there seems to be no
further justification for the commandments themselves.[19] (2)
The philosophical justification of worshipful silence does not
provide the laws ordaining prayer with a religious, or
theological, justification. (3) The Besht's and R. Arele's
doctrine of silence before God may throw an entirely different
light on this problem.

It is, after all, striking that all three use several phrases as
if they were quoting from one another: "in time of trouble,"
"thinking alone," "do not pray," "do not implore God's help." If
this is a valid connection, then what Maimonides was
addressing himself to was not the institution of prayer as
such. How could he have done so in the consciousness of
Judaism? What he was talking about were not anti-liturgical
but extra-liturgical situations. He, like his hasidic successors,
had in mind not the usual situation, but the one which is
"superlative" or extreme—*in extremis*. He was saying: in
times of real anguish, it is ideally conceivable, and perhaps
even desirable, that a prophet might arise who would invite
men to abstain from all material concerns or expressions, and,
instead, silently, desperately to throw themselves on the
mercy of God.[20]

IV.

"When Saint Louis, the king of France, decided to make a
pilgrimage to the holy places, he heard the call of holiness of
Brother Aegidius, and resolved in his heart to visit him at
home. When, for this reason, he came to Perugia during his
travels, where he had heard that the Brother resided, he
went, like a pilgrim poor and unknown, to the gate of the
Brothers and ardently asked for the holy Brother Aegidius.
The gatekeeper went and told Brother Aegidius that a pilgrim
at the door was asking for him. Through the holy spirit

Aegidius immediately knew who it was. Stepping out of his
cell as if drunken, he came to the gate, running fast, and the
two fell into a wondrous embrace and, kneeling, kissed one
another with great fervor, as if they had known one another
like the oldest of friends. When they had given one another
signs of ardent love, neither spoke a word to the other, and,
preserving silence in every way, they parted.

"As Saint Louis was leaving, the Brothers asked one of his
companions who this man was who had been in such ardent
embrace with Brother Aegidius. He answered that it was
Louis, the king of France, who had wanted to behold the holy
Brother Aegidius while on a pilgrimage. Whereupon the
Brothers complained and said to Brother Aegidius: 'Oh,
Brother Aegidius, why did you not want to say anything to
such a great king, who came from France to see you and to
hear a good word from you?' Brother Aegidius replied:
'Dearest brothers, do not be surprised that neither he could
say anything to me nor I to him, for, as soon as we had
embraced, the light of divine wisdom revealed his heart to me
and mine to him. Standing in the eternal mirror, we learned
with perfect consolation what he had intended to say to me
and I to him, without the noise of lips and tongues, and better
than we could have spoken with the lips. And had we wanted
to explain in vocal sound what we felt inwardly, such speech
would rather have bestowed melancholy than consolation
upon us. Thus you may know that he left hence wondrously
comforted.'"[21]

V.

With the exception of the passage in which Maimonides
states his philosophical reason for silence before God, we have
spoken up to now of silence which is caused by man's inability
to put into words his innermost and truest concerns. There is,
of course, another reason for keeping silent before Him, as
Maimonides, in that passage, makes clear: God is so great
that He cannot be compassed in words. Zecharaiah 2:17:
"Keep silent, all flesh, before the Lord, for He is awakened

from His holy dwelling." Habakkuk 2:20: "And the Lord is in His holy sanctuary; keep silent before Him, all the earth!" (When the lion comes roaring out of his lair, no other animal dare raise its voice; and when he is asleep in his lair, the other animals are hushed for fear of waking him.) This truth found its classic expression in the talmudic story of the man who stood before R. Chaninah and appealed to God as "the great, mighty, awesome, powerful, potent, feared, strong, valiant, enduring, honored God." R. Chaninah waited until he had finished, and then scolded him for having heaped so many attributes on the Name of the Almighty. "Even the three attributes which we do declare, if Moses our teacher had not used them in the Bible, and if the Men of the Great Assembly had not come and fixed them in our prayer, we would not employ them."[22] The entire chain of Jewish "negative theology," climaxing in Maimonides himself, finds its basic text in this statement. In Kabbalah, the ultimate name of God is, therefore, *ayin*, "Nothing."[23] Also in the Christian mystic tradition, the recognition that no word and "no-thing" are adequate to God, and that, therefore, properly speaking, only silence befits Him, reaches the ultimate point in the sentence of the *Theologia Germanica:*

Now mark: by the Father, I understand the perfect, simple, Good which is All and above All . . . And it cannot be any of those things which the creature, as creature, can comprehend and understand. For whatever the creature, as creature, can comprehend and understand, conforms with its creature nature; it is something, this or that, and therefore is likewise all creature. Now if the simple, perfect Good were a something, this or that, which the creature understands, it would not be All, and in All, and therefore also not perfect. Therefore, we name it also "Nothing."[24]

VI.

Man is thus literally struck speechless. He stands before his God and can say nothing because he cannot address Him before Whom he stands, and he cannot find words with which to express his own concerns. And yet, speak he must, and he wishes to speak. So he prays to be able to pray: "O Lord, open

Thou my lips, so that my mouth shall tell of Thy praise."
Psalms 51: 17.)

This is a paradoxical prayer. It declares: "I cannot pray
unless You cause me to pray; therefore, I pray that You cause
me to pray. But, of course, I cannot, logically, even pray this."
No doubt, due to this dilemma, the additional verse,
Deuteronomy 32: 3, was later inserted, prior to our verse, thus
reasserting human initiative before launching into the
Eighteen Benedictions: "I will call upon the Name of God."
But now we are again confronted with the first difficulty, the
thesis of Psalms 51: 17.[25] The only thing left to do in order to
break out of this "theoretical" circle is to engage in "praxis"
by simply beginning to pray. But, of course, the theoretical
bind is thereby not invalidated. Thus, when the praxis has
ended, the Eighteen-Prayer concluded, the original silence
reasserts itself:[26] "My God, keep my tongue from evil and my
lips from speaking guile. Let me be silent before those who
curse me . . ." The striking superiority, however, of the
synthetical silence of the end over the thesis of silence at the
beginning is that now it is an ethical silence, in relation to
other men, and pacific, while it started out being merely
theological.

Man must speak, in the first place, because he is not the
perfect spiritual being that can act without taking action, or
express himself without speaking words. God may know what
goes on in his heart without it having been articulated, but
man himself would not know it. Our thoughts come into being
only as they are shaped into representative sounds; the
thought does not exist prior to its name. Our emotions, in
turn, are only chaotic and undirected psychic states until they
have been channeled into self-conscious verbalizations.
Indeed, reason is the *logos*. Without the word, there is
nothing, neither man's knowledge of himself nor of God.
Without speaking of it, man could never come to be aware of
his sin nor could he purify himself of it. In this sense, speech
is in fact a concession to man's weakness or imperfection. Or,
to put it more positively, silent mysticism is always tempted
to fall into wild and meaningless irrationality. *Tohu vavohu*

itself was chaos and void until the divine word transformed it into Creation. In turn, man is not man but by virtue of language. In speaking, he becomes God-like.

There is yet another reason why man must speak. Until we have words, we do not even know what it is that we want to say. There is not first the content, and then the form into which this content is poured, but the form produces its own content. Human speech is not like medieval economics in which a man needed a pair of shoes, went to the shoe-maker and ordered them, and then the shoe-maker sat down and manufactured them. It is rather like modern commodity-production, in which the shoe-maker, having made the shoes, instigates the need for them on the part of the potential consumer. Congregations or individuals, left to their own devices, without prayerbook or precentor, would know neither what to pray nor how to pray.[27]

This is why we use the prayerbook. One is asked: how do I learn to pray? There is really only one answer: pray!

Pray other people's prayers. You will appropriate them to yourself by using them and pouring your own personality into them. Do not wait until you "feel like" praying, or until you know how to pray. You never will. This is really a case of "we shall do and then hear." And even if we could occasionally speak without having to use the thoughts and words of others, how shabby and sentimentally self-indulgent such worship invariably turns out to be! "In a sense, our liturgy is a higher form of silence. . . . The spirit of Israel speaks, the self is silent."[28]

VII.

The passage in *Berakhoth* 33b, which we have earlier adduced, declares that ideally silence were more appropriate to the ineffably great God, but that human dependency on language requires concessions, however limited, on this score.[29] Even these concessions can, however, be annulled when the God of history manifests Himself in cataclysmic events which, literally, "leave us speechless." *Yoma* 69b reports that Jeremiah and Daniel, in the face of the first destruction of Jerusalem, could no longer truthfully speak of God as "mighty and awesome." The Men of the Great Assembly—i.e., the Rabbis who determine our practice—restored the phrase, "the great, mighty and awesome God," on the paradoxical ground that it is precisely God's indulgence of His enemies which constitutes His majesty. How else could the world persist? In *Gittin* 56b, the School of R. Ishmael, therefore, speaking of the second destruction of the Temple, interprets Exodus 15:11 ("Who is like unto Thee among the mighty!") as meaning: who is like unto Thee among the silent! (*elim* equals *ilemim.*)[30] Here, then, a new dialectical level has been reached: in the face of unspeakable events, only a self-contradictory mixture of speech and silence—if anything at all—is tolerable.

The Nazi Holocaust is the contemporary extrapolation of the destructions of the Temple. In highly contemporary language, Theodor Adorno, in the "Metaphysical Meditations" with which he concludes his *Negative Dialectics,*[31] reiterates the liturgical ruling of the Rabbis: "Not even silence breaks out of this circle. All that silence does is to rationalize our own subjective incapacity by resort to the state of objective truth, and thereby degrades the truth once again into a lie . . . . No word sounded from on high, also no theological word, has an unchanged right after Auschwitz." The silence before, during, and after the Holocaust is one of the decisive features of our age,[32] and André Neher has crafted an entire impressive Jewish theology of silence out of this condition.[33] What it all amounts to is that man can no longer speak, and he cannot keep silent—he cannot act in any sector of contemporary society, and he cannot abstain from acting. It is quite literally the situation which Reb Arele contemplated—the paralysis of tongue and hand, and the paralysis of paralysis.

When neither "yes" nor "no" is available, perhaps there is nothing—but also perhaps there is "perhaps." Neher can point this up better in French: beyond *être* and *non-être*, there might be *peut-être.*[34] At the height of Lamentations (3:25-30), silence is commended to man, for thus "perhaps there is hope." An entire penitential poem for the High Holy Day period is built around this refrain: *ulai yesh tikvah*—we have nothing to fall back on, neither words nor deeds; thus "perhaps there is hope." In the meantime one waits.[35] Herbert Marcuse knows that, in the "one-dimensional society," there is nothing that one can do without being self-defeating; but he, nonetheless and self-contradictorily, commends action. Adorno, on the other hand, knew that this is irrational, and therefore, commended watchful waiting. (He died, in effect, in the conflict between the high-decibel level of Marcuse's followers and his own low-decibel level.) And the upshot of the *halakhah* for the Eighteen-Prayer comes to this: we bracket the articulation of "the great, mighty and awesome God" between question marks of "may-be," "may it be!" (*ulai—o lo.*)

VIII.

Thus we always find ourselves suspended between the two opposed impulses: we cannot and must not speak, and yet we must; God cannot be addressed, and yet He must be spoken to; man cannot say what goes on in his heart, and yet he does not even exist unless he speaks out.

The paradox cannot be overcome. There it stands, unresolved and irresolvable. Prayer must always tend to fade off into silence if it is to be a spiritual exercise and reach Spirit. Silence must always tend to erupt into prayer and be undergirded by words if it is to constitute the relationship between two persons, whose very essence resides in the fact of Creation, and whose nature is *logos*. You can only try to pursue both goals at the same time. To reach them both simultaneously is the ideal consummation. You declare: "His Name is elevated above all praise and blessing," and, in the same breath, you praise His Name: "Praised is the Lord who is ultimately praised forever and ever."[36] The paradox can be overcome only messianically.[37]

Chapter Nine

ON THE MEANING OF PRAYER

ERNST SIMON

An examination of the meaning of prayer and worship in Jewish experience involves the analysis of several major questions. What is the nature of prayer, and what are its presuppositions? What specific features characterize Jewish prayer? What is the efficacy of prayer, and what dangers does it involve? To what extent and in what ways can prayer be relevant for the modern Jew?

I.

Genuine prayer is based on three presuppositions. They are not psychological but logical or, to be precise, theological presuppositions. The first is a belief in a personal God as the peak of a hierarchically ordered universe. There is a hierarchical order of being in the universe. We can distinguish different levels of being. In the mineral world, terms such as "character" or "personality" are meaningless and inapplicable. Nevertheless, individual stones or mountains do exist, feel and they would lose their specific character if further divided. Hence they can truly be considered *in-dividuals*. The same is true in the world of plants. Here, too, we find entities which cannot be subdivided without loss of identity.

On the animal level of being, however, we also find "character," if character is defined as the sum total of specific dominant qualities which possess a certain constancy. To ascribe character to an animal or a human being is not a value judgment but a statement of fact: we simply mean to say not only that it or he is an individual but that his or its

100

reactions possess a degree of constancy and can be predicted with reasonable accuracy.

On the level of human existence, we speak not only of individuality and character but also of personality. Only human beings can be personalities. The word "personality" is derived from the Latin noun *persona,* the mask which an actor put on for his performance in the amphitheater. This mask had two functions. It served as a sort of loudspeaker in the great arena, and, at the same time, it helped the audience visualize the character played by the man whose voice it amplified—the role to which his voice gave sound. We speak of personality when we feel that a person gives voice to something that lies beneath the visible surface or, more accurately, that is above it and is sounding through him—a meaning which the Latin verb *per-sonare* indicates even more distinctively than the noun.

As personality, man represents the highest peak in the hierarchical order of being within the world. To become a personality is his highest possibility. God cannot possibly be less than the highest peak which human beings may attain. If He exists, and I believe He does, He must be at least as much as I am—He must be a personality. I do not know what kind of a personality God might be, but I believe He is the source of the possibility that human beings have to become personalities. He is sounding the voice that is sounding through the human personality.

A second presupposition of prayer is man's faith that this personal God cares for His children. Everything that happens on earth is important to Him. The chapter of the Bible which tells the story of the Flood that covered the earth in Noah's time contains a significant sentence, "and it grieved Him in His heart." God was sad that He was compelled to bring the flood upon the earth. God cares.

There is a third presupposition. It embodies man's conviction that he has the capacity to turn to God with his praises and thanks without wishing to flatter or bribe Him, and to approach Him with his supplications without wishing to force Him to do man's bidding. Prayer defined as supplication implies that man requests something of God. But man cannot know whether his request will be granted. This point differentiates prayer from magic. In magic man tries to force God to act in accordance with man's wishes—and he may score a visible success. But by trying to force God to do his will, man transforms Him into an idol. A god who can be forced to do man's will is an idol. The danger of magic lies in its seeming success. The successful man pays a heavy price for his achievement: he loses God. An idol can be defined as a man-made object of adoration in which the worshiper adores his own product, be it the product of his hands or the product of his mind. Idolatry is the duplication of the ego—be it the individual ego or the collective ego, as in racialism or chauvinism. Hermann Cohen once pointed out that it is no less anthropomorphic to speak of God's spirit than it is to speak of God's hands. We may commit idolatry even by speaking of God's spirit if this term denotes a concept that originates in man's mind. Authentic prayer addresses itself not to a god we make but to the God who made us. A prayer of supplication is legitimate only if man turns to God with full awareness of God's freedom of decision, prepared to accept the decision—gratefully, should it be positive, but also to accept it, though perhaps with anguish, should it be negative. God may say *yes*, but He can say *no*, too.

Yet the question remains: Why should we praise God? And why should we thank Him? Is He not above our thanks and praises? Aristotle, in a passage which probably refers to Plato, said that "everybody may criticize him; but who is permitted to praise him?" And Goethe expressed the same concern when he said, *Wer einen lobt, stellt sich ihm gleich,* "He who praises another person places himself on the other's level." If there are valid doubts about our moral right to praise other human beings, must our doubts not be much more severe in our relationship with God? Why then do we praise or thank Him?

We praise God because our hearts need to praise Him. Once, when my son was four years old, he happened to see some beautiful flowers and said to me: "Abba, I am happy with

these flowers. What is the proper benediction for them?"
Though a small child, he expressed a universal human
sentiment. Children can love and enjoy flowers just as deeply
as adults can, perhaps even more so. But this child was a little
Jew who had already learned in his parents' home that
nothing is eaten or experienced without a *berakhah*, a
benediction. Hence it was natural for him to seek a specific
Jewish religious formulation to express a general human
emotion.

Prayer and religious observance must, of course, be more
than merely the products of a conditioning process in the
home of one's parents. They must be rooted in a deeply felt
and affirmed conviction—a conviction expressed, for instance,
in a beautiful saying of the Talmud, "He who enjoys anything
of this world without a benediction is likened to a man who
robs the sanctuary." The Talmud Yerushalmi makes the point
even more strongly when it says that a *berakhah* is the price
we pay for being permitted to enjoy this world. To thank God
and to praise Him is our acknowledgment that God is our
Creator and the Creator of the universe.

II

Prayers and benedictions acknowledge God as man's
Creator; supplications address themselves to God as man's
judge. These definitions apply not merely to Jewish prayer;
they characterize prayer in general. However, Jewish prayer
possesses additional aspects and features which give it its
specific and distinctive character.

First, Jewish prayer is communal prayer. Friedrich Heiler,
in his monumental work, *Das Gebet*,[1] emphasizes that the
Jews were the first people to introduce communal prayer.
Jews can and do pray in solitude, but if they do, they are
expected to recite their prayers at the same time at which the
community worships. We require the presence of a *minyan*, of
at least ten adult males, for many of our prayers, and every
minyan, in turn, is representative of the entire Jewish people
standing before God in prayer. The element of peoplehood

occupies a legitimate place in the framework of our faith.

Second, communal prayer must be formulated prayer. Judaism recognizes that there is a tension between individual and group prayer, between spontaneous and fixed prayer. Prayer can and should be *avodah she-balev,* service of the heart. Judaism knows individual, spontaneous prayer, for prayer must be able to express what is in *your* heart, not in somebody else's. According to Jewish tradition, a Jew may speak or listen to God as his heart may dictate.

But man is not only an individual. He is a participant in his community. He is a member of the Jewish people. Hence, as Milton Steinberg put it, it is not enough that he address God in his solitariness.[2] Prayer, for the Jew, is also *kiyyum mitzvah,* the fulfillment of an essential commandment, which requires him to pray at specified times and in accordance with the specific order of a preestablished text. Communal prayer is formulated prayer.

The third distinctive quality of Jewish prayer can be found in the way in which it employs a multitude of external symbols for internal meanings—the *talit,* the phylacteries, the *shofar,* the *succah, lulav* and *etrog,* Sabbath candles, the spice box for *havdalah.* Other religions use symbols, too; but only in Judaism has "ritual" become a way of life, designed to sanctify every act and stage of man's life, to evoke a constant awareness of God's presence, to discipline man's thoughts, ácts, and emotions, and to relate the Jew to his people's past as an ever-renewed contemporary experience.

The fourth quality which characterizes Jewish prayer is its equation of study and worship. Jewish prayer has an intellectual dimension: the study of Torah is a regular and integral part of Jewish worship even on weekdays. If we turn to the *God of creation* in our prayers of gratitude and praise, and if, in our supplications, we address ourselves to the *God of justice,* to God as our judge, in the study of Torah, we invite the *God of revelation* to speak to us through His words and their explanations. In all other forms of prayer we speak to Him; by studying Torah we listen to what He says to us.

III

Prayer opens up new dimensions of experience to the worshiper. However, it also involves dangers. One danger can be described in the words of Isaiah:

And the Lord said: Forasmuch as this people draw near,
And with their mouth and with their lips do honour Me,
But have removed their heart far from Me,
And their fear of Me is a commandment of men learned by
   rote;
Therefore, behold, I will again do a marvellous work among
   this people,
Even a marvellous work and a wonder;
And the wisdom of their wise men shall perish,
And the prudence of their prudent men shall be hid.[3]

Isaiah raises the fundamental question of *kavvanah*, man's spiritual intent and concentration in the act of prayer. Its lack can seriously threaten the meaningfulness of prayer. Even a deeply pious Jew will rarely be able to say all his prayers with real *kavvanah*. All of us, and the most pious persons perhaps even more than others, occasionally succumb to the danger of praying by rote. Martin Buber, in criticizing the way in which the Torah is frequently read in some synagogues, once spoke of the *Aussatz der Gelaeufigkeit*, "the leprosy of fluency." This leprosy of fluency threatens organized prayer, too. Prayer must be alive, not the mechanical mumbling of words. Routine destroys *kavvanah* and transforms prayer from a dialogue with God into the mechanical fulfillment of a routine assignment.

There is a second danger. The worshiper may be so smugly satisfied with the fact that he is praying that he forgets before whom he should be standing in prayer. He does not speak or listen to God while he prays. He listens to himself. His prayer becomes a performance in which he himself is the audience. This attitude may lead to a third danger, the danger of competitiveness and exhibitionism in prayer. The worshiper begins to compete with his neighbor. What counts is not a person's *kavvanah* but whether he prays more, louder, longer, or in a more conspicuously intense fashion than his neighbor. This exhibitionism destroys prayer: you think neither of God nor of your own feelings in the presence of God; you think of your neighbor.

These dangers are very real, but they do not vitiate the efficacy of prayer and its capacity to open up a new dimension of experience. We may not be able to meet God in prayer. But prayer makes it possible for us to reach the meeting point between God and man, the moment—that point in time— when the I encounters the great Thou. We cannot reach more, but this point we can reach. And in the rare moments in which we are able to reach this meeting point, we reach beyond ourselves.

One can train oneself to pray and to avoid the dangers of rote and exhibitionism. A young man, now a strictly observant Jew, for many years felt unable to attend a *minyan* even on Shabbat. When I asked him one day to accompany me to the synagogue, he refused and said, "How can I pray in the synagogue? I have not yet learned to pray by myself." He has learned it since then. Prayer is one of man's greatest but also most difficult arts. Nobody forces man to pray. But if he wishes to pray, he must learn the art of praying. And one of the ways to learn it is to direct our *kavvanah,* our spiritual concentration, toward a specific theme or thought among the many themes that are embodied in our prayers. I cannot think of any benediction or prayer which, although formulated and fixed by past generations, could not become topical for me or a fellow Jew in a moment of personal or historic import.

More than a hundred years ago, the leaders of Reform Judaism in Germany eliminated the prayers for Zion and Jerusalem from their prayer books. They felt these prayers had become outdated and irrelevant. One rabbi is reported to have gone so far as to transform *Tisha be-Av* into a day of rejoicing. According to Jewish tradition, the Messiah was born on the day the Temple was destroyed—*Tisha be-Av.* The civic emancipation of the Jews was proof to this rabbi that the Messiah had arrived or was about to arrive. Hence, he felt there was no longer any need to pray for his coming or to mourn the destruction of Jerusalem. *Tisha be-Av* could become a day of rejoicing. The notions and emotions of the past had become meaningless to him and his followers. They felt the forms and formulations of the past contained nothing that had topical relevance to their own lives and experiences.

Yet there were other Jews, often simple people, far less educated or sophisticated than the leaders of Reform Jewry, who prayed three times a day, "May our eyes behold Your return to Zion." Some of these men may also have doubted the validity of some traditional beliefs. Others may have recited their prayers by rote. Yet these men were among the people who reclaimed Eretz Yisrael and rebuilt it and saved it for the Jewish people. These men may have lacked the capacity to analyze the text and composition of the prayer book critically and in accordance with the principles of historical scholarship. But they had a feeling for the historical reality of the Jewish people. The text spoke to their hearts, if not to their minds. It was related to their understanding of themselves and their experiences as Jews. It continued to speak to them. It affected their thinking, their actions, their orientation to life.

Many prayers can have a similar relevance to our lives. Therefore I would be extremely careful before I would change the formulations of our prayers. But every Jew should be sufficiently trained to be able to concentrate his *kavvanah* on that theme within the established prayers that is closest to his heart and concerns. He may want to omit other themes, yet the time may still come when some of them return to him so that he may return to them.

An outstanding example of the way in which a formulation or phrase of the past can be made to speak to the concerns of the present is a sermon which Rabbi Nehemiah Nobel, of Frankfurt am Main and one of the great spiritual leaders of German Jewry at the beginning of the century, delivered after he had returned from the Zionist Congress in Karlsbad in 1921. The Congress was torn by a bitter conflict between religious and labor Zionists. Chaim Weizmann had tried in vain to restore unity. Rabbi Nobel, himself a member of the Mizrachi delegation, succeeded in resolving his own inner tension when, preaching at the first Shabbat service after the end of the Congress on the words of the prayer book, "Who healest the sick of Thy people Israel," he transformed the traditional text into a moving and compelling prayer for Weizmann who "was sick with the sickness of the Jewish people." The text was traditional, but in Dr. Nobel's skillful and inspired approach, it revealed a new depth of meaning and relevance. Nobody who heard the sermon will ever forget it. We are not Nobels, but we can probe the text and seek to discover its meaning and applicability in the same way. Our prayers, though formulated by previous generations, have the potency to illumine the predicaments of later generations and to speak anew to the needs of each successive generation. More than is written in them can be found in them.

Personal prayer can also be strengthened by praying with a *minyan*. The impact of a *minyan* upon the depth and meaningfulness of personal prayer was brought home to me by the *minyan* I was permitted to organize in the sickroom of Franz Rosenzweig nearly thirty years ago. Rosenzweig was already too ill to leave his room. He could no longer move around and was immobilized in his chair. Several days before Rosh Hashanah I asked him whether he wanted a small group of friends to conduct a holiday service for him in his home. He eagerly consented. We conducted services on both days of Rosh Hashanah in Rosenzweig's room. The next day he asked, in the only way in which he could still communicate—by pointing his finger in the direction of certain letters on the typewriter while his wife attempted to guess what he meant—"What about Shabbat Shuvah?" We continued our *minyan*, first on Shabbat Shuvah, then on Yom Kippur, and from then on every Shabbat and holiday until his death. It was a good *minyan*. It taught us how to pray. The *minyan* had not been organized for this purpose, yet one of its by-products was that it taught many of us to pray. Rosenzweig was too ill to pronounce the *berakhah* over the Torah audibly. Nevertheless, we often called him to the Torah and then brought the

Torah over to him. Rarely can a benediction have been said with such power, vigor, and *kavvanah* as was the silent benediction which Rosenzweig pronounced while bending his noble head.

Prayer fulfills still another function. It can best be described in the words of the prayer book, "Purify our hearts to serve Thee in truth." Every Jewish prayer is a small Yom Kippur. It challenges us to examine our hearts and thoughts. It demands that we question ourselves—whether we have been silent when we should have spoken out; whether we have been selfish when we should have been responsive to the needs of others; whether we have been thoughtless when we should have been sensitive; whether we have pursued the hollow when we should have reached for that which can hallow our life. In this kind of prayer, we do not ask God to do our will. We accept God's challenge to fulfill His will. We confess our guilt and ask Him for strength to purify ourselves.

IV

Can prayer still be meaningful and relevant to the modern Jew? Prayer is the bridge between God and man, but it can also be the bridge between Jew and Jew. *Vetaher libenu* —these words are known to most Jews, if not from the prayer book, then as the text of a *horah*. Even at the time of the greatest estrangement between the *halutzim* and the traditionalists, the *halutzim* could still express in the language of dance what the pious Jews expressed in the language of prayer. From the Torah to *halutziut*, there is a continuous stream of religious consciousness which has bound together all our habitations and generations. Prayer can create a unity of experience which transcends the boundaries of time and space and bridges the diversity of conviction.

Our definiton and understanding of what is or should be true service to God have changed through the generations and will continue to change. Nevertheless, many formulations of our prayer book have demonstrated their elasticity to encompass a variety of definitions and convictions. Indeed, some of our prayers, especially those which have been central to Jewish self-understanding, have never changed. Think of the *Shema*. Neither its formulation nor its role as a formula giving voice to the deepest loyalties of Jewish consciousness through the ages has ever changed.

The meaning and implications of the *Shema* once were the subject of a discussion between Franz Rosenzweig and his teacher, Hermann Cohen, at a time when Cohen, who was an anti-Zionist, was involved in a bitter controversy with Martin Buber, a committed Zionist. To Cohen's disappointment, Rosenzweig, though not a Zionist, sided with Buber rather than with Cohen. When Rosenzweig visited Cohen one day, his host asked him, "What do you find in Buber that you do not find in me?" Rosenzweig answered, "You have only *Adonai ehad*—'our God is one and a unique God.' In Buber I also find the *Shema Yisrael,* the call to the people." For a moment, Cohen was silent. Then he rose, opened his file cabinet and took out the manuscript of what was to be his last book, *Religion of Reason from the Sources of Judaism* (published posthumously), and read a passage to Rosenzweig which revealed that Cohen, too, had finally discovered, in the *Shema Yisrael,* the call to a particular people, Israel, as the bearer of the belief in the one and universal God.

Both aspects are unified in Judaism. The particular and the universal are fused together. The *Shema* speaks to both, to the traditional Jew and to the liberal Jew, to the religionist and to the secularist; and it unites them in the experience of a common past and the commitment to a common destiny. *Shema Yisrael:* we are the people that is to listen. God is *our* God, the God of our people. But this God is at the same time the God of the universe.

The proclamation of God's dominion over the world is not a statement of fact but of trust and hope. We conclude every worship service with the *Aleynu,* and every *Aleynu* in turn ends with the words of the prophet, *bayom hahu,* "on that day God will be One." He is not yet altogether One; He still bears various names. Therefore, the prayer continues with the prophet's words, *ushemo ehad,* "His name will be One." The end of the prayer which we recite at the conclusion of our worship points to the end of time, when mankind's destiny will be fulfilled—the days of the Messiah.

To pray is to turn to God as our creator whom we praise and thank. To pray is to stand before Him as our judge to whom we address our supplications. To pray is to acknowledge Him as the giver of Torah which we are to study. Ultimately, however, every Jewish prayer ends with the *Aleynu* in which we turn to Him as the God of the future which will see mankind's redemption. Thus, prayer is a gate to our living past. As we probe its enduring meaning, it can become a source of power that points to the ultimate goal of man's existence.

Chapter Ten

THE LIMITS OF PRAYER:
A RABBINIC DISCUSSION

GERALD J. BLIDSTEIN

Prayer is a brazen act. For it is impossible to stand before God, blessed be
He, but brazenly. Every man imagines—in one way or another—the
greatness of the Creator: how then can one stand in prayer before Him? For
prayer is a wonder; [its task is] chiefly the assault upon, and the despoiling
of, the heavenly order . . . man comes, wishing to despoil the order and do
marvels. Therefore man must be shameless in prayer.

Rabbi Nahman of Bratzlav

The human experience implied by the act of prayer forms
the core of the modern discussion of worship. For the ancients,
however, the divine and cosmic experience—or the possibility
of the divine or cosmic experience—was an equally crucial
theme. The perenially vexing discussion of God and the world,
which expressed itself in the perennially vexing problematic
of omniscience, predestination, mechanical causation and
freedom, became an experiential dilemma when man rose to
pray. For if the future was fixed—either by divine fiat or
casual ukase—supplication became a vicious joke.

The Talmudic sage contemplating the fact of a totally
powerful God who yet allowed man his freedom would do no
more than state the paradox: "All is foreseen, yet freedom is
granted."[1] But the Rabbinic mind found itself much more
involved with this and similar problems when the content and
validity of a Halachic moment—the moment of prayer—was
to be defined and defended.

It seemed quite obvious that man's right or duty to make a
request of God stood in some relation to what God or nature
had already ordained. Yet what exactly was this relation?
Could man request everything—and was everything then

free, undetermined? Should man perhaps request nothing —because God had already determined the future? Or were there rules to be established, demarking the areas in which God and the world were free to respond and those in which they were bound?

These questions—and, indeed, the following discussion—are offered with a full awareness of the "organic" nature of Rabbinic thought. Nor am I unaware of the folly of emasculating man's encounter with God and the world of all mystery and paradox in order to satisfy the human need for security. Analysis, however, need never be apologized for, especially when it concerns that most analytic of all documents—the Talmud.

II

The Mishnah states:

A blessing is said over evil similar to that said over good . . . but to cry over the past is to utter a vain prayer. [Thus] if a man's wife is pregnant, and he says: "God grant that my wife bear a male child," this is a vain prayer. If a man is on the road [approaching a town], and hears an uproar in the town, and says: "God grant that this not be from my family," this is a vain prayer. . . . A man should bless God for the evil in the same way as for the good. (Berachot, 9: 3-5)

Broadly speaking, the Mishnah maintains a "rational" stance: prayer is in place when the request made concerns events still in the future, but is futile when the event which forms the subject of the request has already occurred. Furthermore, the Mishnah adds, the occurrence of an event is not to be dated by an individual's awareness or experience of it, but by the situation itself: the foetus, in the case cited, is male or female long before the parents "have" a son or daughter, and their prayers should reflect this fact. To fly in the face of this natural event, to importune God for a son or daughter, is both foolish and impious, an arrogant rejection of the world God has made. Man is to bless God for all events, as the Mishnah aptly continues, whether good or bad. Praise alone is man's proper response to the past.

The discussion in the Babylonian Talmud (*Berachot* 60a) reads as follows:

Are prayers then of no avail? R. Joseph cited the following in objection: *And afterwards she bore a daughter and called her name Dinah (Gen. 30:21).* What is meant by "afterwards"? Rab says, "After Leah had passed judgment on herself . . . the child was changed to a girl." We cannot cite a miraculous event in refutation of the Mishnah. Alternatively I may reply that the incident of Leah occurred within forty days after conception. . . .[2] But does such a prayer [i.e., a prayer concerning the sex of a child during the first forty days of its conception] avail? Has not R. Isaac the son of R. Ami said: "If the man first emits seed the child will be a girl; if the woman first emits seed the child will be a boy?"—We are speaking here in a case where they both emitted seed at the same time.

The Talmud grapples, fundamentally, with two polar problems:[3]

1) The widest latitude allowed prayer by natural law; or, can one request of nature that a child conceived male be born female? The Talmud draws the only conclusion that could possibly be drawn from the Mishnah—one cannot pray for a miracle, though one may occur.

2) The narrowest latitude allowed prayer by natural law; an attempt to define, at least in the specific case under discussion, the precise moment at which an event becomes determined and, hence, the power of prayer ends. Here the Talmud concludes that the integrity of the prayer is to be maintained, even if its application must be limited to a gamble in the twilight zone of scientific freaks. Interestingly, the implications drawn from the "scientific" data as to the effect of prayer are unchallenged; there is no suggestion that prayer possesses a potency beyond the scope of the operative natural law.

Obviously, the field still remains free for many perplexing questions, questions the Talmud might have raised but did not. The Mishnah and Talmud have steered a careful, though by no means rigorous, course; they have granted prayer validity in areas not yet determined, and have affirmed the existence of such areas. The two extremes of a world cohering by accident and one bound in eternal chains have been avoided (or perhaps ignored).

In the Midrash *(Bereshith Rabbah 72: 6;* followed closely by Jerusalem Talmud *Berachot ad loc.),* however, a different point of view is presented:

> The school of R. Yannai say: "This Mishnah refers to a woman already on the travailing-stool." R. Judah ben Pazzi said, "Even when she is on the travailing-stool the sex of the child may change, as it is written, 'I went down to the potter's house, and behold he was doing work at the wheels *(avnayyim).* . . . And the word of God came to me saying, O House of Israel, cannot I do with you as this potter . . .? Behold, as the clay in the potter's hand so are ye in my hand, O House of Israel *(Jer. 18: 3-6).'*"

As the Midrash is elsewhere[4] quick to point out, R. Judah ben Pazzi rejects the Mishnah and its implications. The act of request, he argues, always presupposes miracles; indeed is not God a Lord of miracle? Prayer and God are not to be hamstrung by statistics and averages.

Yet despite the seemingly radical stance taken by R. Judah ben Pazzi, he too steers a middle course. He does not advise parents to pray for a change of sex in the children already born them. The logic of his position (though not the logic of his Biblical citation) would, of course, support this course as easily as it supports the course he actually charts: nothing is impossible for Heaven. Apparently, then, neither the logic of cause-and-effect nor the logic of miracle is sound. Rather, the logic of the religious situation becomes crucial; there is still a point at which one must accept the universe, to quote Margaret Fuller—not as Carlyle exploded, "Gad! She'd better," but because God wants one to do so. For R. Judah ben Pazzi this point is reached when the universe becomes part of the human experience, when the child is born.[5]

Whatever the final disposition of these details, it is clear that R. Judah ben Pazzi rejects the "rational" scheme of the Mishnah, substituting for it a rule that is meaningful on a more profound (and more real) level of existence. Nothing stands between man and God; even the sturdy world is constantly under the judgment of their partnership.

III

The sources cited above consider the freedom of the universe from a causal, or natural, point of view. True, it is God who is appealed to—"God grant . . ."—but it is the rule of nature that is challenged. This remains true even after we concede the fact that "nature," for the Bible and Talmud, is a deliberate and wondrous manifestation of the Divine.[6] Yet the same problem can arise with regard to the future as determined not by natural law but by Divine decree.

The Mishnah *(Rosh Ha-shanah* 1:2) states that man is judged on Rosh Ha-Shanah, and that a future of either reward or punishment is then allotted him. But the Talmud contrasts with this idea the statement of R. Jose, "Man is judged every day" *(R.H.* 16a). R. Jose, as the Talmud understands him, claims that an annual judgment denies the dynamic nature of the human situation, and must hence be unjust. The obvious practical difficulties that arise from the concept of annual judgment mirror R. Jose's concern:

Suppose Israel were [in the class of the] thoroughly virtuous at New Year, and scanty rains were decreed for them, and afterwards they backslided. [For God] to diminish the rains is impossible, because the decree has been issued. The Holy One, blessed be He, therefore sends them down not in their proper season and on land that does not require them.[7]

The judgment is formally maintained ("For God to diminish the rains is impossible") but is in truth abandoned. Life, either of the soul or of the body, cannot be placed in a judicial straight-jacket.

The stance of R. Jose has its roots, then, in the affirmation of divine justice and the disavowal of metaphors and analogies which, while concretizing the act of judgment, bestow upon it the frailties of the human sphere from which they are drawn. For divine justice must be dynamic justice; it must be molded to the ever-changing moral and spiritual contours of the person upon whom it is delivered. The tension between the developing human life and a fixed verdict, unresponsive to a man's subsequent degeneration or improvement, made this latter concept unworkable. Hence R. Jose replaces the weight and magnificence of an annual verdict with the quiet mystery of a daily one.

From a different point of view, the problem is one of the tension of two orders, the irruption of sacred time into secular time, the contrast of man's ability to alternate between Sabbath and the weekdays and his inability to live in both at the same time; indeed, the inability of man to apprehend rationally the structure of such dual time.[8] For while all the days of the week live by the power bequeathed them through the Sabbath, and indeed attain reality through it (as we number our days, "The first day [of the Sabbath]"), the time of Sabbath itself is localized and does not directly enrich or influence the time of the days of the week. The time of the Days of Judgment, however, by imposing its verdict on all the days of the year, days with duration and life of their own, becomes a violation of their integrity. In essence R. Jose cannot admit the tension of these two times, nor can he explain it. Thus, Me'iri, attempting to reconcile the Mishnah and R. Jose, must conclude, "it is all true to those who comprehend."[9]

The Talmudic discussion further probes the opposition of R. Jose and the Mishnah:

R. Joseph said: "Whose authority do we follow nowadays in praying for the sick and for the ailing? That of R. Jose. It is also possible to say that it is after all that of the Rabbis [of the Mishnah], according to R. Isaac. For R. Isaac said, 'Supplication is good for man whether before the decree is pronounced or after it is pronounced.'"

The first alternative claims that the judgment of Rosh Ha-Shanah, if it is real at all, must be totally real; the Divine decree must be final, or it is meaningless. It must be, and indeed is, beyond appeal. A prayer of request is possible only in the scheme of R. Jose; for the Mishnah, God's sovereignty has silenced prayer for the sick and ailing.[10] The second alternative declares the power of prayer unlimited; even after the Divine decree has been issued it must be appealed, and man, who must presume to pit his voice against the decision of Heaven, can succeed in this appeal. God leaves Himself free to respond to man's request whenever it is made, and to man's life as it is lived. The Talmud here declares the Mishnaic position to be an affirmation of the tension rather than the excision of one of its poles; the Talmud does not, however, resolve this tension, or undertake to show how a verdict that must of necessity be subject to instant review and revision is indeed a verdict. These alternatives are a crystallization of centuries of discussion and thought.

The *Sifre*[11] assembles the following contrasting couplets of Biblical verses, among others:

1) *O Thou hearest prayer/Unto Thee all flesh doth come (Psalms* 65: 3).
   Thou hast covered Thyself with a cloud,/So that no prayer can pass through (Lamentations 3: 44).
2) *The Lord is near unto all that call upon Him (Psalms 145: 18).*
   Why standest Thou afar off, O Lord? (Psalms 10: 1).
3) *Seek ye the Lord while He may be found (Isaiah 45: 6).*
   I will not be sought out by you (Ezekiel 20: 3).

These verses reflect, of course, some of the agonies of life. But how are all these verses to be affirmed? The *Sifre* answers that the first verse in each pair describes God before He has issued His decree—the second, after He has issued His decree.

This answer, which was enunciated by R. Joshua ben Hannaniah *(Niddah* 70a) and R. Akiba *(R. H.* 17b), is rational and tough. It offers a "scientific" solution to the gnawing presence of rejected prayers—prayers which need not imply the absence of God but only the power of his administrative prerogatives. The structure of the world makes certain prayers futile at the outset—this is a fact to be accepted. The practical relevance of this approach is seen quite clearly in the following *baraitha:*

R. Meir used to say: "Two men take to their bed suffering equally from the same disease, or two men are before a criminal court to be judged for the same offense. . . One escapes death and the other does not. Why . . .? Because one prayed and was answered, and one prayed and was not answered. Why was one answered and the other not? Because one uttered a perfect prayer, and the other did not." R. El'azar, however, said: "The one man prayed before his final sentence had been pronounced in Heaven, the other after his final sentence had been pronounced." (R. H. 18a)

But while the approach of R. Joshua, R. Akiba and R. El'azar is rational and tough, it may seem to some a betrayal of God's mercy and love, His eternal readiness to accept prayer. Will God be a prisoner of His own decree? Hence R. Meir (at least by implication)[12] cannot accept this answer, which would let the prayer of man vanish, a sacrifice to the realistic mind, and would have God abandon justice to the demands of administrative efficiency. The perfect prayer will be answered, he claims; the rejected prayer deserved its dismissal. R. Meir must eliminate the automatic injustice dispensed by the proponents of the "decree" theory; as is the case with all idealists, he exchanges injustice for either mystery or chaos.

R. Isaac pursued this path to its ultimate conclusions —"Supplication is of value both before the decree and afterwards." He even went so far as to echo R. Jose, saying, "A man is judged according to his present state alone."[13] Finally, he said (as we all do, in part, on the Days of Awe): "Four things destroy the decree against a man: charity, supplication, a change of name, and a change of deed" (R. H. 16b).

These two points of view with regard to prayer (and, incidentally, with regard to t'shuva—return—as well; cf. the discussion of R. Yohanan, Abaye and R. Papa, R. H. 17b) and the Divine decree provide a parallel to the two points of view developed in the discussion of prayer and natural law above. In both instances, the problem is the freedom left in the world, which in both cases is measured by the worth and effectiveness of prayer. In both instances, one body of opinion is willing to fix a point beyond which prayer is futile and the world determined, while another body of opinion preserves the unbounded integrity of prayer and the vitality of justice.

For some, the world is held together by a Divine structure, for others, it is held together by God himself.[14]

Chapter Eleven

THE EFFICACY OF PRAYER[1]

DUDLEY WEINBERG

How did you choose your tie this morning? What considerations determined the selection of a maroon silk tie rather than a woolen one with yellow polka dots against a bright green background?

This question must seem almost indecently irrelevant to our present concern with prayer. But keep the question in mind. We shall return to it and may discover that the selection of a tie is not altogether unrelated to the experience of prayer.

We are asked to think about the problem of the efficacy of prayer.

Questions about the efficacy of prayer would almost never have been asked by the generation of my grandparents. Nor, for that matter, are such questions asked very frequently today with any sense of vital urgency. My grandparents would not have asked about the efficacy of prayer because they prayed as naturally as they breathed. They would probably no more have questioned the efficacy of prayer than they would have questioned the efficacy of breathing. If they had been forced to say why they prayed, they might have responded in some such way as this: "A person breathes to keep his body alive; a Jew prays to keep his soul alive. That's all there is to it." By and large, however, they felt no need to ask the question. They simply prayed.

Our own generation and the children we have raised generally do not ask the question either. But the absence of the question from the list of our primary concerns is due to quite different reasons. Our ancestors did not ask because

121

they *prayed*. We do not ask because we do *not* pray. One does not ask serious questions about irrelevancies—and on the whole, prayer is irrelevant to the concerns of most people in our time.

It is true that some people still *recite* prayers, but comparatively few people *pray*. Those who do not pray at all do not discuss the efficacy of prayer except by way of pronouncing a patronizingly tolerant or arrogantly contemptuous judgment upon those who do. Those who pray (or recite prayers) only occasionally and casually, expressing a marginal rather than a central concern in their lives, do sometimes ask what prayer is expected to achieve. It would be interesting to know what prompts their question. Is it a wistful feeling that they have lost something precious? Or a creeping sense of guilt at having defaulted on an honorable obligation? Is it perhaps an anticipatory excitement about the as yet unexperienced possibilities of genuine prayer—the sort of excitement one feels when planning a trip to faraway places or upon actually approaching the shore of another continent for the first time? Or is the question about the efficacy of prayer prompted by a desire to do missionary work, to persuade someone else that prayer is desirable, enjoyable, productive?

Why do we ask? We could learn a great deal about ourselves if we understood the motive that prompts the question.

We also need to know *what* we are asking. What do we mean when we ask about the efficacy of prayer? We know what we mean when we inquire about the efficacy of advertising, or the efficacy of golf lessons, or the efficacy of medical treatment. Such questions presuppose a clearly desired result. If the action or procedure produces the desired result—if the advertising produces an increase in sales, if the golf lessons improve our prowess on the links, if the medical treatment cures the ailment—we say that it is efficacious; it works.

Are we quite certain that we know what we mean when we ask about the efficacy of prayer? We had an experience of prayer this morning. We prayed in accordance with the

discipline of the Sabbath liturgy. Were our prayers efficacious? Did they *work?* Did they produce specific, measurable,
results which we had hoped for in advance?

As I put these questions, I feel uneasy and almost unclean.
My uneasiness is prompted by the conviction that there is a
sense in which it is offensive to inquire about the efficacy of
prayer, as though prayer were an investment from which we
expect to reap dividends. We might as well make pronounce-
ments about the efficacy of love and tell our children that if
they love, they will make a million dollars or will be certain to
avoid malignant disease. A man loving and in love does not
ask about the efficacy of love. A man in passionate pursuit of
truth, no matter how tormenting and all-consuming his task,
does not ask about the efficacy of truth. But unfortunately,
our judgments are so profoundly affected by the contemporary habit of measuring values according to a pragmatic,
results-getting standard that we often forget that there are
vital areas of human experience which cannot be usefully or
meaningfully considered from that point of view.

We cannot begin to understand prayer until we realize that,
at least in certain respects, prayer is not a cause from which
consequences are to be expected. *Prayer is not essentially a
means of producing results. It is a result itself.* We do not
resort to prayer, at least in the ideal, in order to achieve
something beyond prayer. On the contrary, if we understand
what prayer is, we do a number of other things in order to
achieve prayer. We meditate, we study sacred texts, we
compose liturgies and set them to inspiring music, we
establish regular occasions for worship. We do all these things
and more because prayer itself *is* our goal.

There have surely been moments when we have known that
this is so. Perhaps this knowledge has come to us when we
have wanted most desperately to pray and could not. Is there
anyone among us who has never cried out in the agony of his
heart, "I wish I could pray! I can't!"

What then is prayer?
Prayer, like love and like truth, is far more than we can

ever say about it. But we can make some skeletal observations about prayer which each of us may succeed in covering with living substance during the course of his own spiritual encounters with himself, with other persons and with the Divine Person.

Whatever else prayer may be, it is minimally *what a man does when he recognizes that he stands in the presence of God.* This is the basic truth about prayer. I am not referring now to study groups in which we speculate and philosophize about God; nor do I have in mind the conversations with our children in which we struggle to demonstrate God's existence to them. I mean the immediately experienced reality of our own position in the presence of God. Either we know this reality or we do not. And what I am saying is that prayer is what a man does when he knows it.

How utterly appropriate is the inscription so frequently inscribed over the ark in our synagogues: *Da lifne mee attah omed*—"Know before Whom you stand." Without this recognition prayer can never occur. Introspection may occur; we may engage in psychological self-examination; we may study liturgical texts and even find them interesting as sources of stimulating ideas; but *prayer* cannot occur. With this recognition, the struggle to achieve more perfect prayer, to sharpen and to deepen our apprehension of the Divine Presence can never cease. If God is not at least as real and as present in our lives as are the human persons whose reality and presence are so sharp that we can love or hate them, then the experience of prayer is simply not possible for us.

Viewed from a somewhat different perspective, prayer—as we experience it in our better moments—is man consciously *becoming* what in fact he already *is.* If this statement seems to contain a paradox, there is nothing I can do about it. Prayer is *awareness*—awareness not only of God but of oneself as well. God is what He is and we are what we are whether we recognize and welcome it or not. Prayer is joyous recognition and deliberate thankful acceptance of what we are.

What is man? He is a creator who is also a creature. (It is

easy to forget that we did not bring ourselves into being.) He is a judge who is also judged. He is a lover who is also loved. The conditions under which genuine prayer occurs include at least an occasional, fleeting awareness of the amazing qualities which we discover in our human selves and in our peculiarly human actions. Perhaps our most important insights about the presence of God are those which we achieve through a heightened consciousness of ourselves.

In any case, it seems clear to me that prayer is what happens, or what can happen, when a human being becomes aware of the *total meaning* of anything he does. I mean that quite literally. Any specifically human act—however trivial, however important—when its meaning is plumbed to the very bottom—becomes an occasion for prayer. The act of choosing the clothes we wear, the whistling of a tune, the painting of a picture, the decoration of a living room, the assertion that a political-economic system will or will not produce peace and justice, the giving of charity, the search for a friend, the effort to love, the struggle to express truth—everything we do as human beings can become the occasion, if we look deeply enough into ourselves, for discovering the creative mystery that strikes awe into the human heart. There is, I believe, a non-human, a meta-human, a *divine* dimension in every human act without which the human act would be impossible. When a man finds out—however he finds out whether through the turmoil of his own experience, or through the guidance of wise and sensitive teachers, or through the influence of the community of faith in which he lives—that his humanity is utterly inexplicable in purely human terms, he prostrates himself in trembling awe before the Divinity who confers his humanity upon him. That prostration and that awe are prayer.

Is this not what we say in the Adoration? *Va-anachnu kor'im u-mishtachavim u-modim lifne melech malchay ham'lachim ha-kadosh baruch hu.* Let us translate this declaration not as the Union Prayerbook "paraphrases" it, but in accordance with what the Hebrew actually asserts. *"We fall to our knees, we prostrate ourselves, and make grateful*

acknowledgment before the King who is the King of kings, the
Holy One, praised be He." *That* is prayer. It is what a man
expresses when, having sensed the total meaning of any
action, even the most trivial, he discovers the divine
dimension in his human act.

Now let us return to that necktie about which I asked at the
very beginning. How *did* you select the tie you are wearing?
What did you have in mind when you chose a tie of precisely
these colors and *this* texture to wear with this suit and that
shirt?

Or consider another situation which is almost as familiar
and not much less trivial. A housewife whose concerns are
fairly standard informs her husband one day that it is time to
redecorate the living room. His unhappy protestations
dissolve sooner or later in the gentle fluids of her artful
persuasion or they are simply shattered by the sheer weight
of her persistence. Decorators are summoned, the allegedly
necessary items are purchased, the walls are repainted, the
sofa is pushed from this wall to that corner, the lamp is moved
from that corner to this wall and other equally subtle changes
are accomplished. The man of the house having now been
exhausted financially and physically, his triumphant spouse
steps back to contemplate the tangible fulfilment of her
dream and with uncontainable joy exclaims, "Oh, it's so
beautiful!" Or, if the project came off badly, she is overcome
with tragic disappointment and in a voice choked with tears
she says, "I so *wanted* it to be beautiful."

How do we get that way? Why should it make any
difference whether or not the tie "goes well" with the suit,
whether or not the living room is beautiful?

What did you really do when you chose a tie of such and
such colors and texture? What precisely did the lady do when
she took a chunk of material called a sofa, put it in a space
called a room and arranged within that space a context of
other objects, shapes and colors? In each of those situations a
human being took the raw materials which were available to
him and by placing them in deliberately selected relation-

ships to one another attempted to create something which had not been there before: *beauty!* These examples of "beauty-making" are admittedly trivial, but for that very reason they are relevant to our concern.

No normal adult would ordinarily consider that in asserting that two plus two equal four he had done anything remarkable. But the apparently trivial act of reckoning the sum of two and two reveals some startling implications when we consider it more carefully. The human intellect is unwilling to rest with such an assertion as "two elephants plus two elephants equal four elephants." It must press on to the larger declaration that two of anything plus two of anything equal four—and to this statement it must add the claim that the statement is *true!* As nearly as our limited intelligence and our passionate concern can manage to distill truth out of our experience, the statement is *true.* Two plus two *do* equal four.

Why should we care whether anything is true or not? Why should it make any difference to us? How do we get that way?

Our moment in history is laden with crisis. Mention such places as Cuba or Berlin or Vietnam and nearly every one of you will expound a course of action which, in your judgment, would solve the problems which are focused in these and other troubled places and restore secure and just peace to the world. Only critical examination of your theory and the advantage of being able to view the present from the perspective of a century or so further into the future will determine whether the President of the United States committed a blunder when he failed to appoint you Secretary of State. But our immediate interest is to know why you should care at all about such matters. Whence your concern about justice and peace, even if your concern is only a passing and casual one? We all came out of the jungle, out of a natural world which knows nothing about such matters as justice, peace and brotherhood. What's wrong with the jungle? Why isn't it good enough for us? The lion and the tiger seem quite content with the jungle. Why, in this world in which all life subsists by feeding on other lives, should it ever have occurred to anyone to declare that nations ought to beat their swords into ploughshares and their spears into pruning hooks? How did we get that way?

Let us project ourselves in imagination back to a time in the history of our planet before there was anything resembling human life on earth. Let us further imagine that in that far-off era a visitor of reasonable intelligence arrived on earth from somewhere in outer space. Do you suppose that such a visitor at such a time, seeing whatever he saw, could have predicted that one day in the remote future there would exist on earth a creature who would come to a place called Baltimore in order to attend a convention of an organization called the National Federation of Temple Brotherhoods—and that he would want to make certain that his tie went well aesthetically with his other garments? Or that one day a being would emerge who would assemble disconnected sounds from here and there and knit them together to make a melody or a symphony? Or that another such creature would take some of the substance he had earned by the sweat of his brow and send it off to help other similar creatures in places like Israel, India or the Congo—creatures whom he had never seen and never expected to see? Could such an extraterrestrial visitor as we have imagined, viewing our earth still unpopulated by man, have foreseen that on a day yet to come a human being would look into the face of another like himself and say, "I love you"—and *mean* it? Could any of this have been predicted on the basis of such physical, chemical and biological data as could then have been gathered? For that matter, can it be deduced from such data as are available to us today?

In the last analysis, it is utterly impossible to "account for" human nature and for those actions which are peculiarly human by means of the same methods which "account for" physical and biological phenomena. Whenever we delve deeply into the nature and the meaning of the most insignificant human act, we enter an area of mystery in which the divine dimension of that act is revealed.

Ultimately it is impossible to evade the question which we

have already asked several times: *how did we get that way?* The fact is that every human being is in some degree an artist, a scientist, and a moralist. His talents in these areas of creative activity may be sharply limited or they may be remarkably productive, but no normal man is without some concern for the values of truth, beauty and goodness. No normal man is utterly bereft of the capacity to love. How did we get that way? What did we do to deserve the talents and the capacities which make us human?

The very formulation of the question prepares us for the answer. *The shattering truth is that we do not deserve them at all and that we could not possibly deserve them.*

Nobody ever earned the right to be able to love. No person ever earned the right to be able to write a poem, compose a symphony, or paint a picture—even badly. No human being ever earned the right to be able to have a concern for his fellow man and the corresponding need to create the kind of society in which that concern could be fulfilled. We earn none of these things. Our human talents come to us not as of right, *but as gifts—as gifts freely given, not as rewards earned.* Which is to say that no human being ever deserved to be human, if by "deserve" we mean that the record somehow establishes our claim to those creative talents that distinguish man from the rest of the known universe. A man's humanity is not the payment of a debt; it is a gift given out of love. This may well be one of the profounder meanings of the Biblical statement, "And God created man in His own image." God graciously, lovingly permitted us to be creators too.

The consciousness that we are loved with a love that prompts such magnificent gifts, with a love so abiding and unfailing that it never withdraws its gifts, inevitably invokes the response that all love and all gifts evoke: the response of gratitude. The expression of that gratitude is prayer.

Isn't this precisely what our liturgy teaches us to express? *Ahavah rabbah ahavtanu Adonai Elohenu, chemlah g'dolah veeterah chamalta alenu.* "With infinite love hast Thou loved us, O Lord our God; boundless is the compassion which Thou has lavished upon us." Infinite because unearned; boundless because unaffected by any prior condition other than God's own intention to love us.

The essence of the matter is that we do not have our humanity as a matter of "rights." The truth is that we have no "rights" before God. We have "rights" before one another, but not before God. Before God we are simply the recipients of infinitely precious unearned gifts. *(It is precisely these unearned gifts which establish our human dignity and give us "rights" in relationship to other human beings.)* The knowledge that this is so is inseparable from the need to express the adoring thanks which is prayer.

But gratitude is not our only response to love and the unearned gifts that love confers. When we are able and willing to recognize that we are loved—and we are not always willing and sometimes we are not even able—we are moved to make ourselves worthy of it. We want to deserve what is given to us undeserved, what is conferred by God on faith, so to speak, through His grace. We may never succeed perfectly in this endeavor, but we desperately desire to succeed. If it were not so, no man would ever feel guilty about anything.

The truth is that all love obligates. The love of a man for his wife, of a woman for her husband, of a parent for a child, of a friend for his friend, of God for His creatures, always places the beloved under obligation. It requires him to struggle to do those things that will justify what love gives to him.

Love becomes law in the life of the beloved. To know ourselves the objects of genuine love is to impose upon ourselves the creative disciplines—the do's and the don'ts —that make us deserving of being loved, that are the mark of the mature man and woman—and to accept them not with an irritating sense of privation or loss, but with a joyous sense of fulfillment. Through law, through creative discipline, we discharge some of our debt; we achieve dignity. We become lovers; we too become givers.

It is an important point to remember and to understand. All love becomes law in the human response. Divine love becomes divine law—and we know it, at least partially, as the laws of art, the laws of science and as the moral law.

Or to put it in more familar terms, God's grace and God's mercy become Torah. Therefore we are taught to say *Baruch attah Adonai noten ha-Torah,* "Praised art Thou, O Lord, who *gives* the Torah." It is important to note that the Hebrew verb here is the present active participle and is not the past tense. God *gives* Torah, not God *gave* Torah. He gives Torah in every present moment.

It is, I believe, necessary and realistic to touch on an aspect of the experience of prayer which the popular mind generally attempts to avoid. It is unpopular to speak of fear in most contemporary religious discussions. Phrases like "the fear of the Lord" are regarded as primitive, unworthy and unsophisticated. Many people prefer that religious talk should display a kind of Pollyanna optimism that disregards many of the realities of which we are aware deep in our own vitals. But the whole truth about our need to be worthy of the unearned love we have encountered includes our fear that our unworthiness may result in the withdrawal of the love on which our very lives depend.

Analogies in the scheme of human relationships are easy to find. How would our children feel if they were convinced that we did not love them? How does a man feel if he thinks that his wife doesn't love him?

The liturgy of the Union Prayerbook, at least in its Hebrew text, is completely aware of the frightening possibility that the divine love which sustains and nourishes our lives and which confers our human status upon us could be withdrawn, especially since its availability to us does not depend upon our own merit. We read in the evening service: *V'ahavat'cha al tasir mimenu l'olamim. Baruch attah Adonai ohev amo Yisrael.* The English translation is not easy to understand. It does not say precisely what the Hebrew text says. The English reads: "O that Thy love may never depart from our hearts. Praised be Thou, O Lord, who hast revealed Thy love through Israel."

Does the English translation mean that we are concerned about the loss of our love of God or of God's love of us? The Hebrew prayer is much less equivocal. A literal English translation would read, "Do not ever take Thy love away from us. Praised art Thou, O Lord, who loves His people Israel."

Two important lessons emerge here concerning the kinds of experience which produce prayer. The first is that the fear of losing the sustaining power of the divine love and the expression of the accompanying desire to be worthy of His love through the doing of His will are prayer.

The second is that love, whether human or divine, is always love for a specific person or a specific people. Love is never known merely as a theoretical ideal or as a philosophical principle. We can *think* about love theoretically, but we can only *know* love as an experienced fact.

When we examine ourselves and our actions carefully, we discover the divine dimension in everything we are and in everything we do. And we know that *this* person, this specific person is loved; that *this* people, this specific people is loved; that *this* humanity is loved. That is why we pray, knowing that our very being is the fruit and offspring of the divine love, "Do not ever take Thy love away from us. Praised art Thou, O Lord, who loves His people Israel." When we speak these words, we articulate our struggle to be worthy of a love that is eternal.

The expression of our longing to be worthy of God's love, to come to deserve it through the doing of His will—that is prayer.

These, then, are some of the circumstances under which prayer, real prayer, can occur. These are some of the conditions that make prayer flow from our hearts and our lips as inevitably and as naturally as water flows from a mountain spring.

And when we have prayed this way, does anything come of it? Is prayer productive? Does it work? May we realistically expect that it should?

Basically, I find the spirit in which these questions are often asked repugnant and vulgar. If these questions mean—and this is what they generally do mean when they are hurled at me as a kind of challenge—that measurable rewards, especially *material* rewards, must be promised in advance as the result of prayer, then I must answer that the questions themselves destroy the very possibility of genuine prayer. They are then pagan questions in the worst sense; they belong more properly to a discussion of magic than of religion. The person whose primary question about prayer is, "What's in it for me?" has already announced his pagan orientation and his preoccupation with black magic—whether he realizes it or not.

Asked in that spirit, the questions assume that if we can somehow learn the correct formula and the correct posture for prayer, we can compel God to give us what we want and that we can force Him to do what we want done. God then becomes a kind of Arabian Nights genie and we become *His* masters.

But if, on the other hand, the questions mean to ask what happens *to* a person or *to* a community when prayer of the sort we have been discussing happens *in* a person or *in* a community, then we may, I believe, make a number of meaningful assertions.

I have said that prayer *is* the goal. It is itself an end, not a means. It is one of the ultimate fulfillments of the human personality and the human community. It needs no justification beyond itself, just as art, science and love need no justification beyond themselves. But in the act of achieving the goal of prayer and in the effort of holding to the goal some exciting and important things can and do happen.

In the first place, the person who prays genuinely becomes more completely human. He rests more securely in his humanity because in the act of achieving prayer he learns that his humanity does not depend upon himself alone. It depends on a source more abiding than he is, more reliable than he is, on a source which is infinite as he is not.

The man whose prayer is a grateful recognition that he is a human being—which is to say that he is a creator, a judge, a lover—by the grace of God, will not so easily forsake his humanity by descending to the level of the animal or by foolishly pretending that he himself is God. The responsibility of being human in an inhuman world would be too heavy to bear if it were ours alone. When we acknowledge in prayer that God is the senior partner, so to speak, in our human enterprise, our fear of becoming and remaining truly human dissolves. A man who prays or who struggles to pray is a man whose humanity is growing toward completeness.

It is a second consequence of the effort to pray that a man achieves *total honesty* about himself and his situation. Never mind what he tells other people about himself. In prayer and for himself, he achieves total honesty. To begin with, a man in prayer knows—he *really* knows—the immense degree of his dependence on God. He comes to understand—and more important, to understand without fear—that in the ultimate sense he owns *nothing.* Nothing at all! Not his business, not his money, not his talents, not his family, not his employees. He does not even own his own life, and certainly not the peculiar capacities that make him human and distinguish him from the rest of creation. Abraham Heschel has observed that the pious man, the praying man sees himself not as the possessor of his life, but as the administrator of his life in God's name.

I wonder sometimes what might happen if all the men who go to business, if all the men who practice the professions, if all the men and women who teach our children, if all the men and the women who make important political and diplomatic decisions, before going to their tasks were to achieve this prayerful insight—that they own nothing in the ultimate sense and that it is foolish and self-defeating for them to pretend that they do.

Prayer has the consequence that through it we understand the *absolute* truth of the Psalmist's declaration, *Ladonai ha-aretz um'lo-o,* "The earth is the Lord's and the fulness thereof." What an enormous act of honesty that is!

It is impossible not to be honest in genuine prayer. Why should anyone lie before God, especially when the God we encounter in prayer is He whom the Torah calls *El emunah,* "The God of utmost faithfulness," the God whose love and whose judgment never cease. Why bother to lie? It is only in prayer that we face the real truth about ourselves, the *whole* truth that includes the ambivalences, the egotism, the selfishness, the anger, the obscene murderousness which stir all too frequently in every one of us. It is only in prayer that we are really able to bear and to deal with the whole truth about ourselves. Only in the total view of our situation which prayer affords can we look at all there is to see about our individual selves and about our world and still find the courage and the strength to go on, because it is in prayer that we become aware again and again of the sustaining, redeeming hope that flows from the divine love.

I do not wish to be misunderstood. My view of the personal dynamics of prayer is not to be taken as an assault upon any of the forms of psychotherapy. Psychotherapy is an important and precious tool—but there are dimensions of truth, of experience and of human concern with which psychotherapy does not involve itself. What I emphasize here is simply that a man in prayer achieves a degree of honesty about himself and his situation which he is unable to achieve through any other means. He knows that the law, the commandment, the judgment which proceed from the divine love (remember that love leads to law) are inescapable, and he faces up to them. He confronts his own arrogance and overcomes it, because when he is in prayer he stands where he no longer needs to defend himself and therefore can tell the whole truth about himself. He no longer needs to establish status for himself—not in the presence of God. His status *is* established. He is his creator's responsible creature. He is his Father's child. Man in prayer is honest. He no longer needs to use arrogance as a defense. He can be humble without being humiliated, because he is loved and he *knows* that he is loved.

Does prayer produce any practical moral results? I believe that it does. It is one of the consequences of our involvement with God in prayer that we come to hunger and thirst after righteousness. How else can we return the love with which we are loved? How else can we understand the meaning of the divine concern that makes us human, except by joyously translating our responding love not into merely sentimental declarations, but into specific acts of justice, decency and kindness? How else can we deal with the whole truth about ourselves, including the nasty part, except by struggling to overcome everything in ourselves and in our environment that attacks our precious God-given humanity?

In prayer, if nowhere else, we express our loyalty to the Utmost and thus achieve a clearer knowledge of our duty. When God's love becomes God's commandment, moral consequences *do* follow—not easily, not without struggle and not without the constant need for revision and rethinking, *but they follow*. And they follow not merely as *knowledge*, as the technical ability to make ethical judgments about theoretical situations and to say what is right and wrong. They follow as the courage to *be* and to *do* what our human nature with its divine dimension requires. The creative effort of prayer moves us from the *knowledge* of the good to the *deed* which is good.

Who would have the courage to sacrifice comfort, convenience, hard-earned money, time, even life itself for a noble and holy cause if somewhere in his experience he had not encountered the divine dimension, if he had not understood that this moment in time is *more* than a moment in time; that it is one of the blossoms of eternity?

In prayer, as we have understood it, we achieve the trust that makes it possible for us to continue to live responsibly and creatively through the doubts, the disappointments, the sorrows, the disillusionments, the barren deserts of uncertainty which our lives must inevitably traverse. Why is this so? It is so because the thrilling excitement of the human adventure—which we now also understand as a divine adventure—becomes greater than the human failures from which we must recover. We may almost dare to say that God trusts *us* enough to risk His creative purpose on our response to His trust. The challenge and the ultimate reliability of the divine love diminish our preoccupation with pain, privation and sorrow and inspire us to persevere in the task of perfecting and completing our humanity in spite of our troubles and our weaknesses.

Finally, in prayer we move toward the achievement of our

ultimate human task: the enthronement of God in our human world. In prayer, if our prayer is real, if it is the kind of happening we have been talking about, we achieve a little more of what we mean when we say, *M'lo chol ha-aretz k'vodo,* "the whole earth is full of His glory." We achieve step by difficult, wonderful, creative step what we intend when we say in the Kaddish—and not necessarily as mourners—*Yitgadal v'yitkadash sh'meh rabbah b'al'ma di v're kir'uteh,* "May His great name be exalted and sanctified in this world which He has created according to His will," even though He be *l'ela min kol birchata v'shirata tushb'chata v'nechemata da'amiran b'al'ma,* "beyond all blessings and praises which we can utter in this passing and mortal world."

In prayer we make God King in the world—the God whom we know through His love, His justice and His mercy as we come upon the divine dimension in every human act.

Such things are achieved, I believe, when we achieve prayer. If this then is prayer, and if indeed prayer is achieved, need we ask about its efficacy? Need we inquire if it works?

Chapter Twelve
FROM TEMPLE TO SYNAGOGUE
AND BACK

ELIEZER BERKOVITS

I.

One of the most far-reaching transformations in the history of Judaism was undoubtedly brought about by the destruction of the First Jewish Commonwealth and the Babylonian Exile that followed. It may be described as Judaism's way from the Temple to the Synagogue. In accordance with Jewish teaching, the Temple was not to be rebuilt anywhere outside Jerusalem. Since the Temple Service could not be practiced anywhere outside the Holy City, a new type of religious service had to take its place. The political conditions of the people effected the emergence of the Synagogue. What was originally the makeshift arrangement of the *mikdash me'at,* the "Little Sanctuary," was turned into one of the most significant triumphs of Israel's religious genius. Thus, the great contribution of the Babylonian Exile to religious history was evolved. What were the salient features of the transformation which was accomplished by the creation of the Synagogue?

The Temple Service was a national institution, maintained by the State. The people paid for it, but they themselves were not actively associated with it. The daily sacrifices were offered by the priests on behalf of the people. The priests were the God-appointed representatives of the people. While the priests went about their duties in the Temple, the people pursued their daily tasks in the fields, in the workshops, in business and trade. God was worshipped professionally by a caste reserved and trained for the task. The average citizen was not expected to be familiar with the Temple ritual. In general, the people were the *Am haarets* and ignorant of the Torah. It was "the lips of the priests that kept knowledge."

It is of course proper to add that long before the destruction of Jerusalem there were developments afoot which pointed to new paths. There was, for instance, the institution of the *Maamadot,* the daily assemblages of selected groups of men who met in prayer during the offering of the sacrifices in the Temple; nor were the priests the exclusive repositories of the knowledge of the Torah all the time. The decisive change, however, did not occur till the Babylonian Exile.

Of necessity, in Babylon prayer replaced the sacrifice. In its manifold consequences this development amounted to a major religious revolution. The sacrifice could only be offered by the priest; prayer was expected of everyone. Indeed, the delegation of one's duty to pray to a priest is unimaginable. Every Jew now became actively associated with the religious service. Looked at from the point of view of the people, in the Temple the divine service was mere ritual; in the Synagogue it became personalized religious endeavor. Religion turned inward toward the realm of individual commitment. Hand in hand with the growth in inwardness went the democratization of the religious life. The priestly caste, the professionals of religion, lost their central significance. Every Jew was called upon to pray and to read the Torah in the synagogue.

No doubt, in the days of the Temple, too, the people took an intense interest in the service. Especially for the Holy Days they would come to Jerusalem from all parts of the country. But in the courtyards of the Temple they were *onlookers;* they were an audience and the priests, the performers. In the Synagogue, the audience was transformed into the praying community.

With deepening inwardness and religious democratization in the Synagogue, Judaism became more and more the responsibility of the entire people. The "professionals" having been dispensed with, the knowledge of the Torah became a national obligation. The vicarious Temple service could rely on "the lips of the priests that keep knowledge"; the personalized responsibility of the religious democracy of the synagogue laid the emphasis on general education in the entire domain of Judaism. Thus, the *Bet Haknesset* led to the *Bet Hamidrash;* the house of meeting became inseparable from the house of study.

It was unavoidable that a new type of a religious leader should arise. As the synagogue differed from the Temple so did the rabbi from the priest. The rabbi did not belong to a caste or a class; he was not a professional. In contrast to the priest, there were no religious duties for the rabbi which were not equally binding on all Jews. If the rabbi distinguished himself through his piety, he achieved something that was expected from every one of his fellow Jews. His learning and knowledge of the Torah might have rendered him outstanding, but only because he realized an ambition which he shared with all the people. The rabbi did not prepare himself for the rabbinate; like any other Jew, he prepared himself for the task of living in accordance with the Torah. For many centuries he was not salaried but earned his living like any other Jew, through farming, as an artisan or in trade and commerce. He most certainly was not a clergyman but the most representative layman of his community. He was the teacher who guided his fellow Jews along the path which they all had to follow together.

Such were the changes that shaped the historic image of Judaism since the days of the First Exile. For many centuries, and for the longest period of its history, Judaism has been Synagogue Judaism.

II.

In modern times, and especially in this country, a turning away from the synagogue to a religious institution that is known as the temple has become a mark of progress. As we have indicated, compared with the Temple of old, the rise of the synagogue undoubtedly meant a radical transformation in the forward movement of Judaism. Does the modern temple lead beyond the synagogue or is it closer to the Temple of old? Does it bring the inherent motives of Judaism to more significant realization than the synagogue or does it show greater affinity to the spirit that prevailed in the Temple service of the distant past? Only the answer to this question can decide whether the temple of our days represents religious progress and is not a throwback to a more primitive form of religious practice.

If language and style are indicative of the spirit that is within a man, as indeed they are, one ought to say that the terminology, the vocabulary, that the modern temple has adopted makes it suspect of regression from the people's religion of the synagogue to the clericalism of the Temple of old. We no longer speak of the *shool* but of the sanctuary; it is no longer the *Bet Hamidrash* but the chapel (Webster says s.v. *chapel*: " . . . LL. *capella* orig., a short coat (cappa); later, a reliquary, chapel (because the building where St. Martin's cloak was preserved came to be called capella"). There is no room in the temple for the modest *Shulhan* of the synagogue; we have the much more dignified altar instead. Everything in the temple seems to have added semantic weight. One does not pray in the temple, one worships; a temple Jew does not look for a *Minyan* to say Kaddish, he visits a chapel to recite a memorial prayer. No one ever sings in the temple but chants. The examples are manifold. The style of the modern temple seems to be reserved for the specific domain of piety. Everything seems to be consecrated and dedicated and set apart from everyday human interest and concern.

This is no mere affectation but reveals the essential quality of a certain type of religiosity. Modern temple Judaism is indeed a thing apart from everyday human existence. As in days of yore, temple Judaism is almost completely limited to the immediate precincts of the temple. It is an island of piety set in an ocean of secularism and materialism. The piety of the temple is unsupported by a living religious reality outside it. The holiness of the sanctuary does not go beyond the symbolic presentation of the idea in bricks and mortar. The altar is the elevating symbol of a sacrifice which is required of no one and which no one is prepared to offer. In the circumstances, style has to be pitched to a high note of solemn dignity. Temple Judaism cannot do without an inspirational vocabulary and consecrated props. Unrelated as it is to a living reality, all its religious emotions and thoughts have to be artificially induced by symbolic architecture and effect-producing interior decoration, by suggestive terminology and synthetic decorum. Everything is stimulated from without, nothing seeks expression from within. Everything is premeditated solemnity and mediated devotion.

On the other hand, the style of the synagogue is matter of fact; its accoutrements are essentially functional and not symbolical. This is due to the fact that the synagogue is an outgrowth of Jewish living. The divine service of the synagogue Jew takes place more outside the synagogue than inside it. The *Bet Haknesset* is indeed a house of meeting, not really different in kind from other buildings; for wherever a Jew may find himself, he knows he is in the presence of God. In the *Shool* too he is only continuing his life as a Jew. To pray to God together with the community is a task not essentially different from other tasks; for everything a man does is done in God's presence. A synagogue is not sanctuary but the convenient place for the community to assemble for prayer. Whatever sanctity there is in the synagogue is in the living community and it originates chiefly in the life Jews lead outside the synagogue. Since the Torah is read in public, it is useful to have a *Shulhan,* a desk on which to place it. As to the altar, it has no place in the synagogue. Sacrifice is not a symbolical concept as it was in the Temple of old and as it is in the temple of our days, but is part of the daily discipline and practice of Jewish living. As Philo already said, the altar of God is the soul of man.

Compared with the Eternal Light of the Temple, even the *Ner Tamid* of the synagogue is only a functional object. As the phrase indicates, the Eternal Light is charged with the symbolism of eternity, which is thought to be most adequately expressed by expensive artistic design. The *Ner Tamid* of the synagogue, on the other hand, is a modest little lamp that serves as a reminder of the light which was kept burning nightly in the sanctuary in Jerusalem. Since it has no function beyond recalling memories of the past, the *Ner Tamid* is hardly ever noticed. It is certainly no symbol of eternity. It is not through "meaningful" lighting fixtures that synagogue Judaism seeks contact with eternity.

Even such an exclusively "religious object" as the *Aron Hakodesh* is essentially functional in the synagogue. In the temple we speak of the Holy Ark, which is usually dramatized by the richest forms of deepest symbolical significance. Little edification indeed may be derived from the actual "reading of the law"; but exquisite design and meaningful artistry of the Holy Ark are extremely helpful in creating a devotional atmosphere. The *Aron Hakodesh,* however, should not be confused with the Holy Ark. The concern of the praying community is with the living word of the Torah. What need, and indeed what use, for Holy Ark symbolism beside the breath of the living spirit of the Torah! The *Aron* is not an archaic Ark, which is useless from a practical point of view. The *Aron* is a chest or a box, in which people keep all kinds of useful objects, books, clothes, jewels and so forth. It has been set aside in the synagogue to place the Torah in it for safekeeping till the next occasion of reading and study. As the grammatical form proves, *Aron Hakodesh* is not the holy chest but the chest of the holy. In the synagogue, an empty *Aron* is useless; in the temple, the inspirational effect of the Holy Ark symbolism would remain potent even if the "Scrolls of the Law" were exchanged for a copy of the by-laws of the temple congregation.

III.

Undoubtedly, Synagogue Judaism does associate the idea of holiness with objects and buildings. However, as the phrase by which these objects are known itself indicates, the

Tashmishei K'dusha receive a degree of holiness from the use to which they are put. As the tools of a purpose that aims at the sanctification of all life, they become consecrated through usage and not through glittering dedicatory exercises. The longer they serve the more venerable they become. The creation of an atmosphere of devotion by means of clever architectonic ideas is unnatural in the synagogue. But if such an atmosphere, a *genius loci* as it were, should exist , as well it may and often does, it could only be as the lingering on of the accumulated memories of the religious life of preceding generations. The sanctuary, the chapel, the altar, and so forth, of the modern temple are appointed to convey a message of sanctity to hesitant hearts. They are at the height of their effectiveness when they are still new; wear and tear undermines the dignity of these kinds of symbols.

The *Alte Shool* was the pride of a Jewish community, which would surround it with love as if the old building were a living being. In our days, an old temple is shunned as casting a reflection on the social status of those associated with it, as if they could not afford something newer and better.

In this connection it may be appropriate to make some observations on the subject of religious art as well as religious symbolism. Notwithstanding the efforts that are being made to bring beauty to temple buildings and their interior appointments as well as to bestow artistic value on the religious objects used in the temple, the results are often disappointing and at best of questionable quality. And how could it be otherwise? Beauty is truth because, as Plato saw it long before Keats, it mirrors in the world of material objects a vision of the soul. It is always an ideal, a truth, alive first in his soul, that the artist attempts to impart to his material. Religious art stems from a religious vision, from a religious faith that is intense enough to long for expression. In Judaism the expression of the vision was sought preeminently in living. The aesthetic needs of the Jew were better satisfied in the dynamism of beautiful deeds than in the static harmony of beautiful forms. Nevertheless, it was unavoidable that the spirit that used the *Tashmishei K'dusha* should become reflected in them in aesthetic form as well. Wherever the vision of the soul touches the world of things, beauty is born. The art of the synagogue, which had a long and significant history in the old Jewries of Europe, made visible the reality of religious inwardness in the life of the Jew. But whence is genuine religious art to come in the modern temple? Where is the religious vision, where the overflowing religious faith straining for artistic expression, where the religious reality from which new artistic concepts may emanate? Of course, for money one may always buy the services of outstanding architects and reputable artists. But unlike the cathedral builders of the Middle Ages, these modern temple builders are not as deeply inspired by faith that the religious truth which dwells in their souls could stimulate them to creativity in the field of religious art. Occasionally, they may incorporate in their designs some abstract idea of a personal metaphysics, which may even be admired by the initiated members of the congregation as one admires a museum exhibit. At best, the architects and the artists will copy; they will imitate old synagogue motifs or new church designs. Alas, only all too often the final impression is that of expensive glitter and tinsel. When a modern temple grows old it becomes indeed a shabby thing.

Not altogether dissimilar is the value of temple symbolism. Great religions often cannot do without symbols. When the spirit of man beholds a supreme reality which it cannot name articulately, symbols may be justified. Even though their status in Judaism is questionable, man's need for them may be readily acknowledged. When the religious person has exhausted all his resources trying to express the truth he knows, he may use symbols to hint at the transcendental being which he cannot or dare not address in a manner commensurate with its essence. The symbols of the temple, however, stand in a religious vacuum no less than its art. They do not point from the highest rung of religious awareness at that which lies beyond our reach but hint timidly at what ought to be expressed in human life and which the modern Jew does not care to bring to realization.

The sanctuary, the chapel, the altar, the eternal light, the
Holy Ark, the entire "consecrated style," are substitutes for
religious living. As temple art is mainly tinsel, so are temple
symbols essentially makebelieve.

The symbols of the temple are calculated to evoke
devotional reaction from the worshipper; the tools of
sanctification in the synagogue, however, reflect the living
purpose of the spirit that uses them. Symbolism proposes to
elicit religious meditation from without; sanctification proceeds from within man to the external world of objects and
places. The one is as distinct from the other as is religious
ritual from religious living. It is of the very essence of the
ritual that it employs places, objects and gestures attempting
to make an impact on the realm of the spirit. Religious living
on the other hand, begins in the innermost recesses of the
spirit of man and strives to impart its purpose to the realm of
outside reality. Temple Judaism, unsupported as it is by
religious living outside the temple, is ritualistic. In essence it
is nearer to the cults, charms and incantations of primitive
religions than to the revolutionary transformation that the
synagogue accomplished when it made Judaism the posses-
sion of all Israel.

IV.

The ritualistic nature of temple Judaism finds its clear
manifestation in the most significant feature of temple
architecture. The basic architectural difference between
temple and synagogue is that whereas the synagogue has a
center, the temple has none. In the center of the synagogue
stands the *Shulhan* or *Bimah*, the place for the *Shaliah
Tsibbur* as well as for the reading of the Torah in public. It is
natural for the praying community to organize itself around a
central point. It is in the midst of the people that the word of
God comes to life and it is from its midst that the prayer of all
ascends. The *Shaliah Tsibbur* is not "leading us in prayer"; he
is the unifying focus through which the numerous individual
prayers are woven into the prayer of the community. The

synagogue is essentially a *round house*. The Temple of Jerusalem was a long structure. The courtyard faced the sanctuary, the sanctuary looked toward the Holy of Holies. The more important points of interest were in front of the less important ones. This was a natural arrangement, as it is always where the few perform for the many, as in the theater, the lecture hall, the political meeting place. The stage, the dais, the platform are logically in front of the spectators. In all these cases the "long house" is the structural sign of the inner purpose. So it was in the Temple of old, where the priests performed their duties on behalf of the people; and so it seems to be in the temple of our own days. The place of worship has reverted from the *"round house"* to the *"long house."* The important points of interest have been moved to the elevated platform in front of the congregants. It is there that, like some mystery cult, the essential parts of the service are enacted by the initiated functionaries of the temple. The congregants are in the main audience; as in the Temples of old, they have once again become onlookers. It is true that the professionals of the cult make desperate efforts to encourage the onlookers to become participants. However, participation remains forever vague, colorless, and superficial. It dies away completely as soon as the goading and coaxing directives from the "platform" come to an end. The religious democracy of the praying community of the synagogue, with its immediacy and great moments of spontaneity, is lost. The ugly interruptions of the temple service by the continuous announcing of the pages in the prayer book, decorously performed by the religious experts on the platform, has become part of an ideology. It is indicative of the secrets of a ritual with which only the initiated few may be familiar.

There is no way from the temple to the *Bet Hamidrash*. As in times of Jewish antiquity, once again the religious officials have become the repositories of all knowledge about Judaism. The religious experts of the modern temple are known as rabbis, which however is a misnomer. Judged by their functions and specific status, they are much closer to the priests of bygone days than to the rabbis of the synagogue.

They are the professional keepers of the mysteries; they are like intermediaries, long since abolished in the synagogue, between the people and their God. It was unavoidable that the modern temple should have revived the archaic custom of clothing its functionaries in priestly vestment. In the synagogue the rabbi wears the *Tallit* like anyone else in the congregation; in the temple the religious functionary is marked out by the clerical garb. Unlike the rabbi, he is not one of the community but one set apart from the rest of the people.

One hears a great deal these days about Judaism being a way of life. The truth of course is that for the overwhelming majority of modern Jews, Judaism is not a way at all but ceremony reserved for specific occasions. It is not the case that the modern Jew—as he likes to flatter himself—is anti-ritualistic. On the contrary, he is ritualstruck. With a sense of self-righteous superiority he cuts himself loose from the traditions of his people and from the faith of his fathers; but with what childish self-forgetfulness does he not delve into the mysteries of the secret ritual of his lodge! The same Jew who unperturbed by his abysmal ignorance of all things Jewish, easily dismisses religious practices as mere ceremony, will with a deep sense of gratification deck himself out with masonic insignia and perform the prescribed ceremonial with a solemnity and earnestness worthy of a Corybant. Our temples, too, are the veritable breeding grounds of new-fangled ceremonies and rituals. Never before have Jews indulged so intensely in candle lighting as they do today. A candle-lighting ceremony never lets you down. Numberless are the variations of the initiation-of-new-members ceremony as well as of the installation-of-new-officers ritual. No self-respecting temple will be without the dedication-of-the-first-year-students-of-the-Hebrew-School celebration. The consecration service ritual is usually prepared, rehearsed, and enacted by the modern Jew with hardly less devotion than that with which his ancestors were wont to observe the Sabbath or, perhaps, even Yom Kippur. Except that with the modern Jew it all starts and ends in the temple. It is all

solemn and symbolic but unrelated to real life and therefore
superficial—a mere phantom.

V.

Is, however, our analysis not belied by the religious revival
which seems to be sweeping American Jewry? Unfortunately,
all the characteristic marks of faith and piety are lacking in
this revival. In all our magnificent temples one would look in
vain for the "broken spirit" and the "contrite heart," without
which one may hardly find one's way to God. There is no
convincing sign of the modern Jew's willingness to submit to
God, of his preparedness to accept the *Ol Malkut Shamayim,*
the yoke of the Kingdom of God, which is to be established on
this earth. The religious concepts of *Yirat Shamayim* and
Ahabat Hashem, of the fear and the love of God, are foreign
to him. One discerns very little respect indeed for the
authority of the spirit and the relevance of its standards for
the life of man. The modern Jew's revived interest in Judaism
is sociological and psychological; it has little to do with
religion proper.

Strangely enough, the reawakened interest in Judaism is
often a sign of assimilation. Within the climate of American
culture, religion has become a sign of respectability. For some
mythical reason an atheist is not considered a trustworthy
citizen. And so Jews, caught by the fever of conformity,
remembered that they too had a religion. Since, however, to
have a religion is essentially a matter of social convention, it
is sufficient to have it symbolically, without going to all the
trouble of making it a way of life in earnest. One respects
conventions in order to show that one belongs to the class of
"the right people," but to overdo it would be in bad taste. It is
an observation worth pondering that whereas in the ghettos
of former days one could meet occasionally a convinced
Apikoros, in American Jewry one hardly ever comes across a
genuine atheist. We are all believers because religion is no
longer for us a matter of vital conviction but a mere mark of
social status. We are as religious as we are inclined to

conform to the standards of our middle-class mass-culture. We shall be justified in looking for religious revival when American Jewry will produce its own articulate atheists. It will be a sign that religion has ceased being a matter of indifference and has gained sufficient interest to be worthwhile rejecting. Our present affirmations are of little religious significance. We do not confess God but give a nod to the social convention that it is proper to confess a God, some God, any God.

Psychologically our religious revival is to be a cure-all for our anxieties. Religion has become a substitute for the couch of the psychoanalyst. It is expected to give us peace of mind, to bring us happiness, to guarantee us good health, and to assure us of never-ending prosperity. This religion is not God oriented but man centered; man is not required to serve God, but God is meant to serve man. It is the typical religion of a comfortable middle class. We have everything now: jobs, professions, homes, cars, insurance policies; and we also *have* a God. It is useful to have a God; one can never tell when one may need him. Our religion is a prop for our prosperity and comforts. No one is concerned with the word of God; no one listens and no one obeys. The function of our awakened piety is to confirm us in our habits and our customary way of thought. We believe in God, but we also limit his authority. We prescribe for him how to act toward us. Truth for him is what *we* hold to be true; right what *we* consider right. He can ask of us no more than what we ask of ourselves. Most important of all, he is to be considerate; in no way may he inconvenience us or interfere with our comforts and pleasures. The essential quality of this religiosity is that man does not practice what he believes but believes what he practices. We believe in God after having shaped him in our image. It is a religion cut to measure to suit us. It is not a way of life but a means to affirm to ourselves our own way of living. And since our way of living is basically secular, it is the misuse of the sign of the spirit in order to lend security and dignity to the materialism of our concept of life. It is religion without any significant spiritual content. It represents a rejection of the authority of the spirit and an attempt to transform it into a magic force to be harnessed to the drives of our self-seeking.

The quality of our religious revival illustrates the motivating impulse behind the regression from synagogue to temple. Because the main function of religion has become to confirm us in our way of living, and since no interference with our life practices may be tolerated, Judaism has been relegated back to the precincts of the temple and limited to specific observances of specific occasions. Because the authority of the spirit is rejected, one may admit only symbols of the spiritual. Since the modern Jew is concerned only with the effects of the symbols, all that is left is ritual and ceremony. Before there may be any new religious growth in our midst, we shall have to find our way back to the position which was attained by us when we moved on from the Temple to the Synagogue. We have a long way to go.

Chapter Thirteen

GOING TO SHUL

MILTON HIMMELFARB

In the past months, since my father died, I have been in the synagogue twice a day to say the Kaddish. Other congregations would regard mine as observing bankers' hours, but its morning schedule nevertheless requires arising in the dark and cold, especially in the winter. For afternoon-and-evening prayer the hour varies, depending—at least in principle and in Orthodox synagogues—on the time of sunset, but going every evening is not easy, either.

Which is why not even the devout necessarily frequent the synagogue every day, contenting themselves with private prayer, particularly on weekdays. It is the man who is saying the Kaddish who must have a *minyan*, public worship. In most American synagogues nearly everyone you see at prayer during the week is a mourner, together with most of those who are there from the beginning on Saturday morning. Inconvenience also helps to explain the 10th-man problem, quite apart from the big explanations we like better: the difficulty of belief, the difficulty of prayer. In few synagogues where the speech is English and the faces shaven is it unnecessary to have a list of volunteers who can be telephoned in an emergency in order to round out the required number of ten.

In the Middle Ages it was thought that saying the Kaddish for a year was especially helpful to the dead if they had been wicked. Since no one wanted to imply that his father or mother had been wicked, today we say the Kaddish for eleven months. I do not know what proportion of Jewish men observe the full eleven months, but I suspect it is fairly high, especially when put beside our known propensity for staying away from the synagogue.

If this is so, why? Well, feelings about death, especially the death of a parent; guilt and anxiety, and the need to relieve them; ritual—all these can be interpreted along conventional Freudian lines and have been, often. For Freud, religion was a kind of public, collective neurosis. I take this idea seriously. It tells me better than anything else why the very inconvenience of saying the Kaddish morning and afternoon-evening every day for eleven months, and thereafter on anniversaries—normally at least two in a man's life—becomes a virtue, perhaps an attraction. It is expiatory, it is almost punitive, and we have been taught that guilt seeks punishment.

It is more, of course. Much has been said in dispraise of Jews who obey the rules of the Kaddish though otherwise they hardly ever pray at all. The contempt is unwarranted: the Kaddish must meet their needs better than anything else in the synagogue. And these are not only needs of the kind we have learned about from Freud, but also needs for style and tradition. Freud said that the collective neurosis of religion spares us the trouble of developing individual, personal neuroses. With the Kaddish, Judaism spares each Jew the trouble of developing for himself a style—etiquette, ritual, mode of expression, symbolic action—at a time when he wants it and when he knows he cannot devise something personal that will be as good.

If each of us were accountable for his own ritual of mourning, who would escape censure? Who would escape his own censure? The Jewish rites—the burial, the seven days at home, the Kaddish—have the advantage of being a tradition, a style. We need assume no responsibility for them, as we would for any personal or private symbolic action, nor can there be any question of their appropriateness. They are appropriate almost by definition, because of their antiquity, their near-universality, their publicness—*quod semper, quod ubique, quod ab omnibus.* Yet their publicness, so far from making them exterior and impersonal, makes them all the more appropriate to the particular relationship between mourner and mourned: the Kaddish I now say for my father, he said for his; and so back through a recession of the generations that exceeds what my imagination can grasp. Acting as my father acted, I become conscious that I am a link in the chain of being. Nor am I hindered from expressing particular, local, present emotion.

One of the things a Jew is supposed to say about someone who has died is the prayer that Abigail said for David (though in his lifetime and in his presence), that his soul may be bound up in the bundle of life. Saying this is of a piece with the rest of our ritual. Whatever its efficacy may be for the dead, it binds *me* up in the bundle of life, situates *me* in the procession of the generations, frees *me* from the prison of now and here.

Although we have been born when it is hard to believe in immortality, the Kaddish helps us to believe, a little. I know that it makes me think of my father often, more than forty times a week; and it will keep reminding me of him after I have stopped saying the Kaddish daily, when I hear someone else say it and I make the appropriate response. To think of my father, to recall him, is to hold off his mortality—and because ritual is eloquent, to hold it off still one generation further. Where has Daddy gone? To shul, to say Kaddish for Grandpa. By doing what allows my children to ask this question and receive this answer, I also allow myself to hope that my own mortality will similarly be delayed.

A Kaddish-sayer and shul-watcher can learn something even if his experience, like mine, has been limited to not many more than a dozen synagogues, Orthodox and Conservative, mostly in or near New York.

With our past and present confusingly simultaneous, many of us are not in the category we should be in. Of the elderly and immigrant, for instance, it is to be expected that they will use a Polish-Russian Ashkenazi pronunciation of Hebrew; of the middle-aged, the standard Ashkenazi that was taught in our Hebrew schools a generation ago; and of the young, the more or less Israeli, more or less Sephardi pronunciation that is now taught in most schools—for instance, *yitbarákh,* "may (he/it) be blessed": standard Ashkenazi, *yisborákh;* Polish-Russian, *yisbórekh, yisbúrekh.* With eyes closed, you can usually know the man by his Hebrew. Usually—but I have opened my eyes after hearing *yisbúrekh* to see a youngish man who could be in advertising or public relations. And as with pronunciation, so with the atmosphere and the ways of a synagogue. In any synagogue you are apt to find people who by all the rules belong more properly in a different one.

Jews who are americanized (or anglicized, or gallicized; before Hitler, germanized) want restraint in their synagogues, in the officiants as well as the laity. The virtuoso cantor, I had thought, came into his own at a certain time in history, when Jews from the traditionalist villages were moving to the big cities of Europe and America, and he disappeared when their children learned that his kind of singing was out of place in a church. I have not heard really gaudy *hazzanut* anywhere recently, but I have heard other survivals from the bad old days where there was no reason to expect them: a kind of falsetto throating; stretching or repeating some words and swallowing others; singing as if the text consisted of vowels alone, without consonants.

If bar-mitzvahs are a horror, as everyone says, they are normally not so in the synagogue itself. That may come later, somewhere else. But even so, the accumulation of bar-mitzvahs, two or more a week, week after week, can be too much of a good thing. By now I can do without the high voices, and the slow chanting, and the charge to the boys, and the congratulations to the parents, and the benediction, and the presentation of kidddush beakers and prayer books, and the boys' pledges and thanks. If I am querulous, put the blame on lingering shock. Not long ago I heard a bar-mitzvah boy double as cantor when the Torah scroll was being returned to the ark. At that point the cantor summons the congregation with a verse from the 148th Psalm: "Let them praise the name of the LORD, for His name alone is exalted." Instead of *yehalelu et shem,* however, the boy sang *yehallelu . . . ,* "Let

them profane the name . . ."! (The identical phrase is in
Leviticus, negatively of course: ". . . that they profane not
My holy name," *we-lo' yehallelu et shem qodshi.* "Profanation
of the Name," *hillul ha-shem,* is the rabbinical term for
blasphemy specifically or conduct unbecoming a Jew
generally.)

Sometimes I wonder about the bar-mitzvah guests. The
occasional woman in a sleeveless, near-decollete dress
—where does she get her notions of seemliness? The uncle for
whom the Hebrew blessings are practically nonsense syllables but who accepts being called up when the Torah is
read—why does he do it? Since his abject stammering is
surely as painful for him as for the rest of us, he might at
least rehearse the syllables a day or two earlier.

In my wanderings I have discovered an argument, new to
me, against the Orthodox segregation of the sexes. It is still
true that when women sit by themselves they talk, and in
shul they have to be shushed—one of the few things our
grandmothers have in common with their college-graduate
granddaughters. When in a Conservative synagogue and
dispersed among the men, the same women seem to talk less
than when in Orthodox isolation. After one deafening
Sabbath morning near the divider between the men and
women, I could appreciate the answer of the great Rabbi
Israel Salanter—I think it was he—when he was asked what
should be done with some bricks left over from repair work on
a synagogue: "Use them to wall up the entrance to the
women's gallery." In a way, that is what Conservative and
Reform Judaism have done.

I have a research project for a specialist in the social
psychology of small groups: examine a daily *minyan.* It is an
ideal opportunity for a participant-observer, especially if you
have to move about from time to time and so get to see how
others are.

Take the *minyan* in the congregation I belong to. When you
consider that its members are unhappy about having to be
there in the first place and that its composition changes,

veterans departing as newcomers enter, its morale is remarkable. On the whole they are not conspicuously pious Jews, but most make it a point of honor to disregard bad weather and hazardous driving to get there on time. Clearly they believe that the *minyan* must go on, that it would be wrong to let the side down.

So strong is this sentiment that it makes some who have finished their eleven months keep coming, if not every day then one or two mornings during the week. That is when it counts, because Saturdays and Sundays are no problem. Getting up early when they want to sleep a little longer, and could, their own daily Kaddish-saying now behind them, they show a devotion and self-sacrifice more to be respected than the writing of a check or the signing of a petition. These men do the inconvenient thing so that the other men, who need the *minyan,* will have it. And though they may be too bashful about this motive even to admit it to themselves, I suspect they do it, too, because of what they think a shul should be: a place from which the praises intoned by Israel ascend, as is said of the *Shema'*, "evening and morning, twice every day always, lovingly"—or thrice, if you take the afternoon prayers (which lack the *Shema'*) and the evening prayers to be separate in fact as well as principle.

I have the impression my *minyan* is something of an exception in its morale. At any rate, I find it more attractive than others I have seen. It has little of the prevalent mumbling combined with sprinting that is another survival from the bad old days. In my *minyan* we sing. Not only that, but also I can actually finish one prayer before the next is begun. We are out at the same hour every day, because it is the starting time that varies, not the leaving time: we start early on Mondays and Thursdays, when the Torah is read, and earlier still on a New Month. With the time for leaving calculated and fixed, we do not race the clock. For the kind of people we are, the singing and the deliberate pace ratify our being engaged in what we recognize as suitable prayer. It may even make us a little more prayerful than we would be otherwise.

Not many of us have or attain *kawwanah*—inwardness, concentration, the merging of the pray-er with his prayer. They say it used to be common. Whether or not that is so, I can hardly recite a verse of six or seven words without my mind wandering. (I can hardly listen to three bars of music at a concert without my mind wandering.) Beside *kawwanah*, decorum and singing and pace and every other occidental propriety are trash. Unfortunately, though, their absence does not guarantee its presence; and if we are going to have to do without *kawwanah*, we may as well have niceness. Let a man be free enough from haste to be at least aware of the plain meaning of the words he is saying or singing. When he leaves, hurrying to his car, let him not have a bad taste in his mouth.

I still catch myself daydreaming about the things I would do if I were rich. Lately, one of those things has been to have my own shul, with the legislative, executive, and judicial powers all mine. I would make some radical reforms, of a generally reactionary character.

As among the Sephardim, I would have the reader read every word aloud, from beginning to end, except for meditations intended to be silent or those minatory admonitions that are traditionally muted, like Deuteronomy 11:17 after the *Shema'*. As Maimonides decreed for the Jews of Egypt, I would have the Standing Prayer said only once, aloud. Every biblical text that is more than one or two verses long would be chanted, like the Torah and the Prophetical lessons and the Megillot. (The prayer book includes many psalms, but I have yet to hear one chanted that way.) I would have the musical emphasis that is given to a prayer, or even a phrase, correspond to the doctrinal or liturgical emphasis it ought to have. I do not pray for the restoration of the sacrificial cultus, nor does the prayer book I use (on the Sabbath) include a prayer for it; and the Conservative theologians who edited that *siddur* even refrained from translating the biblical prescription for animal sacrifice incorporated in the Standing Prayer for *Musaf*. Yet the congregation is encouraged to sing that very passage, in an almost fondling sort of way: "And on the Sabbath day, two he-lambs. . . ."

The Sabbath service is on the long side: in my congregation three hours—not unusual—and in another I know of, four. The other is the Orthodox synagogue of Sons and Daughters of the American Revolution. It may be that the four-hour Sabbath worship is one of the reasons why the Sons and Daughters stay away from their synagogue so religiously.

The length of the synagogue service, on the Sabbath and festivals and even weekday mornings, is only a sign of the contradiction or tension in our worship. On the one hand, the Rabbis enjoin us not to make a perfunctory routine, qeva‛, of our prayer. On the other hand, our liturgy consists, with some expansions and additions, of prayer texts that the same Rabbis declared to be ḥovah, obligatory. It is hard to keep the repeated and obligatory from becoming routine. Even in the age of faith only a small elite could have succeeded.

But to make the service short will not help us much. I have felt most untouched and unmoved in short services, Reform or near-Reform Conservative or Reconstructionist; and my neighbors have seemed to me equally untouched and unmoved. In fact, length has certain advantages. In a way a long service is like a long poem. You do not want unrelieved concentration and tightness in a long poem; they would be intolerable. Length requires longueurs. A good long poem is an alternation of high moments and moments less high, of concentration and relaxation. In our snyagogues the heights may not be very high, but the long service does provide some ascent and descent. The short service tends to be of a piece, dull and tepid.

If I shortened at all, it would be at the end rather than the beginning—the Musaf, not the introductory hymns and psalms. Time would also be saved by a total ban on bar-mitzvahs (let them go somewhere else), but twenty minutes or so would continue to be reserved for the sermon. The sermon would not be consistently topical, because I can acquire on my own the approved attitudes toward whatever the approved topics may be at any given time, from the approved sources: *New York Times Magazine, Saturday Review,* public-service television. It is less easy to acquire Torah.

My most reactionary radicalism would be reserved for the Friday-night service: back to Orthodoxy, almost all the way. Almost—because I would substitute some other reading from rabbinical literature for *Ba-meh madliqin,* which, besides being boring, is offensive in the reasons it gives for women dying in childbirth. Job should forever have put an end to that kind of theodicy.

How to recruit a good congregation of respectable size is a problem I am unable to solve even in a daydream. A bare *minyan* is not quite right for a Sabbath, let alone Rosh Hashanah and Yom Kippur. "In a multitude of people is the glory of a king." For the Rabbis, that verse from Proverbs proved that Jews should worship together, the more the better. A large number of worshipping Jews assembled together can generate a kind of heat—analogous to the physical heat that people generate when they are closely assembled—that will affect each one individually. I have heard about it but I have not experienced it. On Rosh Hashanah and Yom Kippur a large number of Jews are assembled where I go, only most of them are not what anyone would call worshipping Jews. They are there, they bring their warm bodies, but they are a kind of inert mass and they deaden rather than quicken the worship. They are an audience—not an especially understanding one—rather than a congregation. According to Ninotchka, Stalin wanted fewer but better Russians. That is a cautionary precedent, but I would still be glad to exchange some Jewish quantity for quality.

Now, as to the prayer books I would use: something on the order of Birnbaum's excellent *siddur* and *maḥazor,* but different in having an English facing page that does not give the impression it was written by a hand in a woolen mitten. (For Ps. 24: "The earth is the LORD's and the fulness thereof,"

he has "The earth and its entire contents belong to the LORD.")
Conservative variations should be presented, besides the
Orthodox text. I would not particularly mind additional
readings and meditations from modern work, provided they
were additions not substitutions, and provided I could
continue to ignore them. Either the modern lends itself with
difficulty to what a prayer book should be or editors have
usually made the wrong choices—probably both. A warning:
if "insight" appears anywhere in the book—except perhaps in
the introduction, and preferably not there, either—I will not
buy it.

A good *siddur* is particularly useful during those necessary
and soothing low-keyed stretches in the service. You may
decide, for instance, to read a psalm or a rabbinical prayer
more closely than you could if you were trying to keep up with
the cantor and congregation. You can read for anything you
wish—plain meaning, literary effect, doctrine, allusion or
suggestion, historical placing, or even praise and supplication. If there are good notes and a good translation, you have
most of the help you need.

For astigmatics like me, make sure the Hebrew characters
are large and distinct, and more especially watch those vowel
signs: I often have trouble telling a *qamez* from a *segol* or a
patah from a *zere*. To Hebrew editors and printers everywhere
I commend the example of David de Sola Pool in his edition of
the Sephardi prayer book, who for short *qamez* uses the
left-hand half of the sign. Unlike the Ashkenazi, the
Sephardi-Israeli pronunciation distinguishes between long
and short *qamez*, and a visual marking of the distinction is
something to be grateful for. Without it, in hard or doubtful
cases it becomes necessary to see whether the Kittel-Kahle
Biblia Hebraica has a *meteg*, for example; and then what if
the verse or word is not biblical? But even Dr. Pool is not to be
completely relied on in these difficulties, because the
Sephardi *siddur* is far from identical with the Ashkenazi.
What is more, the Sephardim's tradition is unacceptable
about such matters as the length of the *qamez* preceding
hatef-qamez: for instance, instead of *tohorah*, "purity," they

say *ṭahorah,* and Dr. Pool so points it.

My *siddur* would go to the Sephardim for variety, as in the Kaddish. The Kaddish is a doxology, of which the substantial and historical kernel is the congregation's response: "May His great name be blessed/praised (forever and ever)." Formally, it is not a prayer for the dead; only the graveside Kaddish mentions the dead, and then not specifically but generally, in its praise of God as the future author of resurrection. The four forms of the Kaddish said in the synagogue—two by the cantor or reader, two by mourners—are, as it were, punctuation marks in the service, setting off one part from the next. As far as "may He establish His kingdom" the Ashkenazi Kaddish is the same as the Sephardi one; but then the Sephardim (and Hasidim) add, ". . . causing His salvation to spring forth and bringing near [hastening the advent of] His Messiah." Why not take that over into, say, the reader's Kaddish *Titqabbal* or the mourner's Scholars' Kaddish? It would make somewhat more explicit the messianic hope that the Kaddish has expressed from the beginning.

In the *Kedushah,* with the reader repeating the Standing Prayer and reader and congregation saying a doxology built around "Holy, holy, holy," there are slight differences between the Ashkenazi and the Sephardi-Hasidic texts. Every now and then we might want to follow the Sephardi usage, and the *siddur* ought to have it for us. In the *'Alenu* we should take from the Sephardim the passage that the Christian censors deleted from our text.

The story is told about a Hasid—the same story in its essentials no doubt exists in other religious traditions, too—that people complained of his frequent absence from the synagogue. "I start to go," he told them, "but when I leave the house I see God's world testifying to the majesty of Him who in His goodness renews every day, continually, the work of creation. So I recite some psalms, like 'The heavens declare the glory of God,/and the firmament proclaims his handiwork' and 'How great are Thy works, O LORD!/Thy thoughts are very deep!' And then, by the time I remember where I am and where I was going, it's too late, and I don't get to shul. But," he said, brightening, "sometimes I don't get distracted by thinking about God, and then I go."

Does the moral apply to us? Of course, but not entirely. We are different from that Hasid. We do not bless the Creator for His creation, because we have learned that the argument from design is a fallacy. Both for him and for us the synagogue is a distraction, but for us the distraction is unlikely to be from thinking about God.

Another story about Hasidim: In the presence of their sleeping master, two disciples were talking low about how hard it was to resist temptation, and how the *yeẓer ha-ra'*, the Evil Desire, kept running after them. Their master, who had not been asleep after all, opened his eyes and said: "Don't flatter yourselves. The Evil Desire isn't running after you, you haven't reached that height. You're still running after the Evil Desire."

Even when a man has arrived at a high degree of spirituality, we are informed, he has problems. I suppose an analogy might be with the rich, who have problems that the poor are either ignorant or skeptical about, and certainly in no position to complain about. The frail spirituality of the synagogue must be a real problem—for the spiritually rich. Who will believe us, paupers and groundlings, if we pretend that it is our problem and that we have reached that height?

NOTES

Notes to Chapter One

1) Cf. Hyman G. Enelow, "Kawwana: The Struggle for Inwardness in Judaism," in Hyman G. Enelow, *Selected Works.* Vol. IV. 1935, pp. 252-288.

2) Don Isaac Abravanel, *Yeshu'oth Meshiho.* Jerusalem, 1967, p. 14a.

3) Deuteronomy 9: 18.

4) Numbers 12: 13.

5) B. *Shabbath* 115b.

6) Ismar Elbogen, *Der jüdische Gottesdienst.* 4th edition. Hildesheim, Georg Olms, 1962, p. 8.

7) *Mishnah Abhoth* 2: 1.

8) B. *Sanhedrin* 105a.

9) *Mishnah Abhoth* 2: 13.

10) *Mishnah Berakhoth* 4: 4.

11) B. *Berakhoth* 29b.

12) Abraham Joshua Heschel, *Man's Quest for God.* New York, Scribner's, 1954, pp. 64ff.

13) B. *Berakhoth* 29b.

14) *Sepher Abudraham.* Prague, 1784, p. 30a.

15) B. *Berakhoth* 34a.

16) B. *Berakhoth* 16b.

17) *Ibid.*

18) *Ibid.*

19) B. *Berakhoth* 17a.

20) Cf. Elbogen, *op. cit.,* p. 124.

21) Philip Birnbaum, ed., *Daily Prayer Book.* New York, Hebrew Publishing Co., 1949, pp. 103-117.

22) Cf. S. Baer, ed., *Seder Abhodath Yisrael.* Berlin, Schocken, 1937, p. 91.

23) Cf. Birnbaum, *op. cit.,* p. 377.

24) *Ibid.,* pp. 237-247.

25) *Ibid.,* p. 605.

26) Cf. L. Landshuth, *Ammudé Ha'abhodah.* 2nd edition. New York, Hermon Press, 5725, Appendix, pp. x-xiii.

27) Cf. A.A.Wolff, *Die Stimmen der ältesten glaubwürdigsten Rabbinen über die Pijutim.* Leipzig, 1857; and Leopold Zunz, *Die Ritus des synagogalen Gottesdienstes.* Berlin, 1859, pp. 162-173.

28) Cf. *Seder Rabh Amram Hashalem,* ed. Frumkin. Jerusalem, 1912, Vol. II, p. 172b.

29) Cf. Robert Gordis, *Judaism for the Modern Age.* New York, Farrar, Straus, and Cudahy, 1955, pp. 195-203.

Notes to Chapter Two

1) B. *Ta'anith* 2a.
2) Maimonides, *Mishneh Torah, Hilkhoth Tephillah* 1: 1.
3) *Ibid.*, 1: 2-3.
4) *Ibid.*, 1: 4.
5) *Ibid.*, 1: 5.
6) Cf. Jakob J. Petuchowski, ed., *Contributions to the Scientific Study of Jewish Liturgy.* New York, Ktav, 1970, pp. 1-177.
7) Deuteronomy 6: 7. Cf. B. *Berakhoth* 2a.
8) *Mishnah Berakhoth* 1: 4.
9) B. *Berakhoth* 4b.
10) Cf. Elbogen, *op. cit.*, p. 102.
11) Maimonides, *op. cit.*, 1: 6. Our italics.
12) Pliny, *Historia Naturalis*, ii, xxxv, 36. 12.
13) Heschel, *op. cit.*, p. 97.
14) Eliezer Berkovits, "Prayer," in Leon D. Stitskin, ed., *Studies in Torah Judaism.* New York, Yeshiva University Press and Ktav, 1969, pp. 119f.

Notes to Chapter Three

1) Leopold Zunz, *Literaturgeschichte der synagogalen Poesie.* Berlin, 1865, p. 23.
2) Cf. Ibn Ezra on Ecclesiastes 5: 1.
3) Psalm 150: 3-5.
4) *Kuzari* II, 50.
5) Psalm 29: 2; Psalm 96: 9; I Chronicles 16: 29; II Chronicles 20: 21.
6) The *Targum* translates: *beshibhhorath qudsha,* which means "in holy splendour," and does not get us much further—although, in essence, this is also the meaning of Martin Buber's modern translation, "im Aufglanz der Heiligung." (*Das Buch der Preisungen.* Berlin, n.d., p. 55.) The LXX has *en aule hagia autou* ("in his holy court"). The Vulgate has *in atrio sancto ejus* ("in his holy hall"). Both versions led Kittel to the conjecture that the Hebrew *Vorlage* must have read *behazrath* or *behadrath qodsho.* The medieval Jewish commentators generally felt no need to comment on this phrase. David Kimchi explains: "You must give God glory and holiness with your words, because *hadar* means 'glory.'" *Metzudath David* comes close to the Greek and Latin versions by explaining: "The place where God is glorified in holiness, that is the Temple." It is the *Be-ur* of the Mendelssohn school which moves in the direction later adopted by most modern translations and commentaries: "With the ornamentation and decoration of holy garments which give glory to those who wear them, and perhaps the priestly vestments are meant." M. Buttenwieser (*The Psalms.* Chicago, 1938) renders the phrase in Ps. 29, "in holy array" (p. 148), but retains "the beauty of holiness" for Ps. 96: 9 (p. 320). W.O.E. Oesterly (*The Psalms.* London, 1939) has "holy array" in both instances (pp. 200f. and 423f.), explaining it to mean "special garments." That is also the sense in which A. Cohen (*The Psalms,* Soncino Press, 1945, pp. 83 and 316) understands the words, pointing out that the worshippers of God "must be suitably attired." The RSV has "in holy array," while the NEB has "the

splendour of holiness" in the text, giving "holy vestments" as an alternative.

7) *Pesiqta deRabh Kahana,* ch. XI, ed. Buber, p. 97a. Cf. the slightly different version in *Pesiqta Rabbathi,* ch. XXV, ed. Friedmann, p. 127a.

8) *Mekhilta deRabbi Yishmael, Masekhta deShirah,* ch. III, ed. Horovitz-Rabin, p. 127.

9) Cf. *Entziklopediyah Talmudith,* Vol. VIII, columns 271-284.

10) Cf. Jakob J. Petuchowski, *Heirs of the Pharisees.* New York and London, Basic Books, 1970, pp. 39-56.

11) Saul Lieberman, *Hellenism in Jewish Palestine.* New York, Jewish Theological Seminary, 1950, pp. 129f.

12) Quoted in *Entziklopediyah Talmudith,* Vol. VIII, column 273.

13) J. Huizinga, *Homo Ludens.* New York, Roy Publishers, 1950, p. 10.

14) Huizinga, *op. cit.,* p. 11.

15) Romano Guardini, *Vom Geist der Liturgie.* 19th edition. Freiburg, Herder, 1957, pp. 53f. (Our translation from the German.)

16) Guardini, *op. cit.,* pp. 57f.

17) Friedrich Heiler, *Prayer.* New York, Galaxy Books, 1958, pp. 344f.

18) Heiler, *op. cit.,* p. 344.

19) Maimonides, *op. cit.,* 1: 1.

20) Evelyn Underhill, *Worship.* New York, Harper Torchbooks, 1957, p. 209.

21) B. *Berakhoth* 26b.

22) Moses Maimonides, *Moreh Nebhukhim,* III, 32.

23) Quoted in Jakob J . Petuchowski, *Prayerbook Reform in Europe.* New York, World Union for Progressive Judaism, 1968, pp. 243f.

24) Romano Guardini, *Prayer in Practice.* New York, Image Books, 1963, p. 10.

Notes to Chapter Four

1) *Mishnah Berakhoth* 4: 4.

2) B. *Berakhoth* 29b.

3) *Ibid.*

4) B. *Berakhoth* 29a.

5) *Mishnah Abhoth* 2: 4.

6) Y. *Yoma* V, 3, p. 42c. Cf. Jakob J. Petuchowski, "The Wayfarers' Prayer," in *The American Rabbi,* April 1962, pp. 16-20.

7) Isaiah 65: 24.

8) B. *Yebamoth* 64a.

Notes to Chapter Five

1) *Mishnah Sotah* 7: 1.

2) Maimonides, *Mishneh Torah, Hilkhoth Berakhoth* 1: 6.

3) *Sepher Hasidim,* chapter 1590, ed. Wistinetzki, p. 389.

4) *Shulhan Arukh, Orah Hayyim* 101: 4.

5) B. *Shabbath* 12b.

6) Cf. Petuchowski, *Prayerbook Reform in Europe,* pp. 84-104.

7) Louis Jacobs, *Principles of the Jewish Faith.* New York and London,

Basic Books, 1964, pp. 95-117.

8) Heiler, *op. cit.*, p. 67.

9) Cf. Birnbaum, *op. cit.*, p. 738.

10) Cf. Birnbaum, *op. cit.*, p. 138.

11) Cf. Elbogen, *op. cit.*, pp. 95ff.

12) Quoted in Petuchowski, *Prayerbook Reform in Europe*, p. 135.

13) Cf. David Philipson, *The Reform Movement in Judaism.* 3rd edition. New York, Ktav, 1967, pp. 168f.

14) Joseph Heinemann, *Prayer in the Period of the Tannaim and the Amoraim.* (Hebrew.) Jerusalem, Magnes Press, 1964, pp. 182ff.

Notes to Chapter Six

1) Robert A. Millikan, *Autobiography.* London, 1951, p. 309; quoted in Louis Jacobs, *Jewish Prayer.* London, Jewish Chronicle Publications, 1955, p. 19.

2) Joseph Albo, *'Ikkarim* IV, 18, ed. Husik, Vol. IV, p. 160.

3) Albo, *op. cit.*, pp. 162ff.

4) *Mishnah Berakhoth* 5: 3.

5) B. *Berakhoth* 33b.

6) Heinemann, *op. cit.*, pp. 158-175.

7) Maimonides, *Moreh Nebhukhim*, I, 95, Pines translation, pp. 139f.

8) *Ibid.*

9) Cf. Naphtali Wieder, *Islamic Influence on the Jewish Worship.* (Hebrew.) Oxford, East and West Library, 1947, *passim.*

10) *Tosephta Berakhoth* 6: 7; ed. Lieberman, p. 35.

11) *Mishnah Berakhoth* 9: 3.

12) B. *Abhodah Zarah* 54b.

13) B. *Yoma* 69b.

14) There are, of course, all kinds of fanciful interpretations of the word *hithpallel* which aim at softening the direct cultic confrontation with God, and which tend to blur the distinction between prayer and meditation. For example, it has been argued that *hithpallel* "really" means "to judge oneself." But all of those attempts do not stand up to the critical gaze of the Semitic philologist. See, for a recent discussion of this question, Edward Ullendorff, "Thought Categories in the Hebrew Bible," in Raphael Loewe, ed., *Studies in Rationalism, Judaism and Universalism, In Memory of Leon Roth.* London, Routledge and Kegan Paul, 1966, pp. 278-281.

15) Cf. Y. *Berakhoth* I, 1, p. 2d.

Notes to Chapter Eight (Steven S . Schwarzschild)

1) This essay has gone through several stages. It began as a meditation for the "Oconomowoc Group," an informal colloquium of Orthodox, Conservative, and Reform rabbis in the 1950's. Part of it was a *debhar Torah* at the Rabbinical Assembly of America, in 1961. The version prior to the present one was published in *Judaism: A Quarterly Journal of Jewish Life and Thought*, Vol. 10, No. 3, Summer 1961, pp. 195-204.

2) For the justification of this translation of a phrase which is very difficult and rarely commented on, cf. S.R. Hirsch, Israels Gebete. 3rd

edition. Frankfurt a/M, 1921, pp. 103-107.

3) Cp. the very instructive article by Leon J. Liebreich, "The Impact of Nehemiah 9: 5-37 on the Liturgy of the Synagogue," in *Hebrew Union College Annual,* Vol. XXXII (1961), pp. 228f. and references.

4) Such a situation does not imply that the two parties have become fused; their respective identities may still remain preserved, in accordance with Buber's insistence that the Jewish mystical experience is not one of *unio mystica.* They continue to confront one another, but they do so within one another, rather than over against one another.

5) The Roman Catholic rosary recitation may be compared to this.—Franz Rosenzweig discusses silence as religious expression in *Der Stern der Erlösung,* Part III, pp. 78-81 (3rd edition) immediately before discussing the liturgy of the Day of Atonement, pp. 81-86 (*The Star of Redemption,* tr. William W. Hallo, New York, Holt, Rinehart and Winston, 1971, pp. 321-328), but he does not actually get around to discussing this last section of the liturgy. One almost has the feeling that he meant to get to it, but just failed to do so.

6) Rosenzweig, *op. cit.* pp. 45f. (= *The Star of Redemption,* tr. William W. Hallo, pp. 295f.). In congregational life, one often meets the person who complains about the monotony and passivity of the liturgy. This is a product of the modernized "dignity and decorum" of the service. If we only rose and sat down, closed our eyes, jumped on our toes, knelt and stepped backwards, held the fringes and let go of them again, etc., as the traditional Jew does,—a football game and a round of golf could not compare with the exhilarating exercise of such a service. By the same token, the Shofar Service, of which we have spoken, has degenerated in the contemporary bourgeois congregation into a vulgar infant's trumpet recital.

7) His biography can be found in *Sepher Uvda de'Aharon.* Jerusalem, 1948—even now a scarce book. Professor G. Scholem thinks that R. Arele was one of the extremely few authentic hasidic leaders in modern times, if only because he did not acquire his position—such as it was—by right of heredity. R. Aharon Rote should be regarded as being in direct line, in general and on the specific subject of silence, with R. Menachem Mendel of Kotzk.

8) *Sepher Shomer Emunim,* 2nd edition, Vol. I. Jerusalem, 5719, chapter "Confidence and Self-Fortification," p. 186b.

9) *Ibid.,* pp. 105a f.

10) There is a distinct anti-medical bias in this book. Cf., e.g., p. 188.

11) *Ibid.,* p. 106a.

12) *Ibid.,* p. 106b.

13) Cf., e.g., E.L. Allen, *Existentialism From Within.* London, 1953, p. 32.

14) *Ibid.,* p. 57.

15) J.P. Sartre, *Existentialism.* New York, 1947, p. 34.

16) *Mishneh Torah,* "Laws of Prayer," 1: 1. It is, in any case, interesting that even here Maimonides goes out of his way to ascribe historico-psychological, rather than philosophical or religious, reasons to at least the number and the form of the prayers. Cf. *ibid.* 1: 4-7, chapter 2, etc.

17) Cf. the classic statement by R. Haninah in b. *Berakhoth* 33b. Compare b. *Megillah* 26a.

18) *Guide of the Perplexed*, Part I, chapter 59.

19) Cf. S .R. Hirsch's attack on Maimonides, in *Neunzehn Briefe über Judentum*, 18th letter.

20) There are, of course, all sorts of gradations of silence, all the way from the silence of emptiness to the silence of overbrimming fulness, from the silence of agony to the silence of ineffable joy. Maimonides' and Rosenzweig's silence, on balance, partakes more of the character of messianic silence, while the Kotzker Rebbe's and R. Arele's silence is very much this-worldly and historic. These are by no means the same. Yet these gradations also cannot be neatly separated from one another, as the similarity of terminology in these two cases illustrates; they blend into one another. It is, above all, important to destroy the facile classifications of "rationalist" and "mystic." Kabbalah and scholasticism share a common biblical and Platonic heritage. It is also interesting to note that, on the scale of silence, Rosenzweig, commonly associated with "existentialist despair," leans more toward messianic silence, while R. Arele and the Kotzker, representatives of Hasidism, commonly associated with this-worldly joy, give expression to the silence of anguish.

21) Translated from Martin Buber's *Ekstatische Konfessionen*, pp. 70f. Aegidius became a disciple of St. Francis in 1208, and died in 1262. The writer, now a citizen of St. Louis, Mo., may, perhaps, dissociate himself from the syndrome of the antisemitic, pietist crusader, Louis IX, and the proto-capitalist role of the Jews in the France of his time.—Cf. J. Parkes, *The Jew in the Mediaeval Community*. London, 1938, Index, s.v. "Louis IX," and his own forthcoming *The Jew Marx*, chapter "Marx's and the Jewish Analyses of Interest."—Friedrich Heiler, in *Das Gebet* (5th edition, Munich, 1923), pp. 288-290 and notes, has collected some other beautiful passages on silent prayer.

22) Cf. note no. 17.

23) Cp. Rashi, Ibn Ezra and Nachmanides to Exodus 15: 11—God is "too 'awesome' for 'praises'."—Wittgenstein's doctrine of silence in the *Tractatus Logico-Philosophicus* (4.115, 4.1212, 5.61, 6.522, 7=Preface, second paragraph) has been traced to Kabbalah by Juergen Habermas, "Der Deutsche Idealismus and die Jüdischen Philosophen" (1961), in *Philosophisch-Politische Profile*. Frankfurt, 1971, p. 49. About Arnold Schoenberg's "Oh word that I lack," cf. S. Schwarzschild, "Theology in Music," *Judaism*, Vol. 10, No. 4, Fall 1961, p. 369. Cf. also Barbara Le Bost, "Silent Transfiguration," *Cross Currents* XVI/3, Summer 1965, pp. 295-304, and the striking short story, "Dr. Murkes Gesammelte Schweigen," by Heinrich Boell.

24) *"Darum nennt man es auch Nichts."* *Library of Christian Classics*, Vol. XIII, *Late Mediaeval Mysticism*. Philadelphia, 1957, p. 347.

25) Cp. Emil L. Fackenheim, *Quest for Past and Future*. Indiana University Press, 1968, pp. 201f.

26) Cf. R. Yoḥanan in b. *Berakhoth* 4b, 9b, 17a.

27) This is even true of, say, a Quaker who prays privately and silently. He would have nothing to say before God if antecedent human culture had not bequeathed to him language and forms of thought which he used internally.

28) Cf. Maimonides, *loc. cit.* Cf. also A.J. Heschel, *Man's Quest for God,* "Prayer begins where Expressions End," "To Thee Silence is Praise," pp. 37-44.

29) Cf. note no. 17.

30) Cf. also Abba Ḥanan's statement there. Cp. *Yalqut Shime'oni, Beshallah,* no. 350; S. Schwarzschild, "The Lure of Immanence," in *Tradition,* Spring-Summer 1967, pp. 93f.

31) Frankfurt, 1966, p. 358; cp. also p. 371.

32) Cf. George Steiner, *Language and Silence.* London, 1967; S. Schwarzschild, "Judaism, Scriptures, and Ecumenism," in L. Swidler, ed., *Scripture and Ecumenism.* Duquesne University Press, 1965, pp. 119ff.

33) *L'Exil de la Parole—Du Silence Biblique au Silence d'Auschwitz.* Paris, 1970; "Speech and Silence in Prophecy" (Hebrew), in *El Ha'Ayin.* Jerusalem, 5729; "A Reflection on the Silence of God," in *Judaism,* Vol. 16, No. 4, Fall 1967.—The philosophic, metaphysical background to Neher's theological doctrine of silence can be found in, e.g., *Le Je-Ne-Sais-Quoi et le Presque-Rien* (Paris, 1957) of his colleague, Vladimir Jankélévitch, a member of the important but all-too-neglected group of contemporary French-Jewish intellectuals, to which also the phenomenologist E. Levinas belongs. Silence is close to identical with "the I-don't-know-what" and "the almost-nothing" of Jankélévitch's title.

34) Cf. *L'Exil de la Parole, op. cit.,* pp. 256-259; *"L'être est corrigé par le Peut-être."*

35) Cf. Isaiah 21: 11f., 30: 15-18, Lamentations, *loc. cit.*

36) This may, therefore, be the true theological reason, not the ingenious Tannaitic interpretation reflected in Ibn Ezra's exegesis, for the liturgical connection between Nehemiah 9: 5 and the *Pesuqe de Zimrah,* as suggested by Liebreich, *loc. cit.,* pp. 236f.

37) An important dimension of the dialectic of speech and silence, namely that of art, cannot here be unpacked. A tentative bibliography out of which it can be put together is: Hegel's "death of art" in the *Philosophy of Art;* Steiner and Adorno, *op. cit.;* John Cage, *Silence.* Middletown, Conn., 1939; Max Picard's turgid *The World of Silence.* Chicago, 1952; Gisèle Brelet, "Music and Silence," in S.K. Langer, ed., *Reflections on Art.* Baltimore, 1958, pp. 103-121; Susan Sontag, "The Aesthetics of Silence," in *Styles of Radical Will.* New York, 1969.

Notes to Chapter Nine (Ernst Simon)

1) Published in English as *Prayer: A Study in the History and Psychology of Religion,* trans. by S.M. McComb (New York, 1958).

2) Milton Steinberg, *Basic Judaism* (New York, 1947), p. 117.

3) Isaiah 29: 13-14.

Notes to Chapter Ten (Gerald J. Blidstein)

1) *Mishna Abhoth* 3: 15. Note also the two contrasting statements of Samuel in b. *Mo'ed Katan* 18b.

2) Some rough edges are still left. For Rab, the sex was *changed;* the subsequent allowance of forty days in which to pray assumes, I think, that

the sex has not yet been determined.

3) I realize that the Talmud's immediate concern is the reconciliation of texts. I am interested in the implications of the discussion in its entirety.

4) *Tanḥuma, Vayeze*, section 8. From the *Tanḥuma* it might appear that the view of the school of R. Yannai was held to be contrary to the *Mishnah* as well.

5) If this is so, R. Judah ben Pazzi does not necessarily reject the *Mishnah, in toto;* he accepts the general principle, "He who makes a request of the past has uttered a futile prayer," and may even accept the example of the man entering the city to the sound of cries. He rejects the specific prayer concerning a foetus.

6) Cf. G. Blidstein, "Nature in Psalms," in *Judaism*, Winter 1964, p. 29, note no. 2.

7) *Sifré*, Deuteronomy, sec. 40. Elsewhere, R. Simeon b. Yoḥai is identified as the author of this statement.

8) Despite a common vocabulary, I am not specifically working within the concept of the mythopoeic perception of time discussed by Ernst Cassirer, Mircea Eliade, and others.

9) *Beth Ha-Behirah* to *Rosh Hashanah*, p. 156.

10) Cf. *Tosaphoth, ad loc.*, and Me'iri to b. *Nedarim* 49a. The expression, "nowadays," is of interest.

11) *Sifré*, Numbers, section 42.

12) The *Sifré*, cited above, carries an alternate view as well: In the one case, Israel is doing the will of its Father in Heaven, in the other case, it is not. Here, too, merit is the cause of judgment. R. Meir himself stated that a man is judged on Rosh Hashanah, and his verdict is sealed on Yom Kippur (*Tosephta R.H.* 1: 13); he thus affirms both realities—that of the judgment of Rosh Hashanah-Yom Kippur, and that of the dynamic reality of justice all year round. In R. Meir, then, we find (at least, according to the talmudic exposition) a paradigm for the harmonization of the *Mishnah* and R. Isaac. We will not seek, however, a resolution of the tension existing between these two realities. A further problem is the identity (assumed as a working hypothesis in this essay) of *gezar din* (decree) in all Tannaitic sources and the judgment of the Days of Awe. Some of these sources might seem to require a different construction.

13) Despite the usual interpretation of the proof-text, R. Isaac's statement (as, perhaps, the proof-text itself) can be taken to refer to both past and future states.

14) The Talmud also distinguished between prayer offered for the community (or with a community) and the prayer of an individual. But it is forced to admit that, despite the wider powers granted community prayer, it, too, can be rejected because of a prior final decree of special dimensions (B. *Rosh Hashanah* 18a). The general willingness of God to suspend his *gezerah* in order to satisfy the request of a righteous man was often noted. Cf. Y. *Ta'anith* III, 10, b. *Shabbath* 63a, etc.

Notes to Chapter Eleven (Dudley Weinberg)

1) Based on the transcript of an address delivered at the Nineteenth

Biennial Convention of the National Federation of Temple Brotherhoods and the Jewish Chautauqua Society, in Baltimore, November, 1962, and published in pamphlet form by the Jewish Chautauqua Society, in 1965. We are grateful to the Jewish Chautauqua Society and to its Executive Director, Mr. Sylvan Lebow, for the permission to reprint this pamphlet in its entirety.

CONTRIBUTORS

GERALD J. BLIDSTEIN—Associate Professor of Rabbinics and Hebrew Literature, Jewish Studies Program, McGill University, Montreal, Canada.

ELIEZER BERKOVITS—Professor of Jewish Philosophy at the Hebrew Theological College, Skokie, Illinois.

ABRAHAM J. HESCHEL—Professor of Jewish Ethics and Mysticism at the Jewish Theological Seminary of America, New York City.

MILTON HIMMELFARB—Editor of *American Jewish Year Book*, and Contributing Editor of *Commentary*, New York City.

JAKOB J. PETUCHOWSKI—Professor of Rabbinics and Jewish Theology at Hebrew Union College—Jewish Institute of Religion, Cincinnati, Ohio.

STEVEN S. SCHWARZSCHILD—Professor of Philosophy and Judaic Studies at Washington University, St. Louis, Missouri.

ERNST SIMON—Professor Emeritus of Education at The Hebrew University, Jerusalem, Israel.

DUDLEY WEINBERG—Rabbi of Congregation Emanu-El B'ne Jeshurun, Milwaukee, Wisconsin.

INDEX